First published 2007

Reprinted 2008

LAST REFUGE Ltd.

Photography © Adrian Warren and Dae Sasitorn

Text © Elizabeth Loving and David Halford

This book was designed and produced by

Last Refuge Ltd.

Batch Farm, Panborough, near Wells, Somerset, BA5 1PN, UK, tel: (44) (0) 1934 712556

e-mail: info@lastrefuge.co.uk, web: www.lastrefuge.co.uk

Designers:

Dae Sasitorn

Will Brett

Front cover: *Chesil Beach, Dorset*
Back cover: *Suilven, Ben Nevis, Bannau Sir Gaer, Corran Ra, Peat Works on Somerset Levels,*
Stonehenge, Maiden Castle, Caerleon Amphitheatre, Castle Acre Castle,
Beaumaris Castle, Hurst Castle, West Burton Power Station, Canary Wharf,
Second Crossing Severn Bridge, M25/M23 Junction
Opposite: *Cheddar Gorge, Somerset*

All photographs in this book are available for publication or as prints from www.lastrefuge.co.uk

ISBN: 978-0-9544350-8-0

Printed and bound by NPE Print Communications, Singapore

BRITAIN
The Mini-Book of Aerial Views
A Journey Through Time

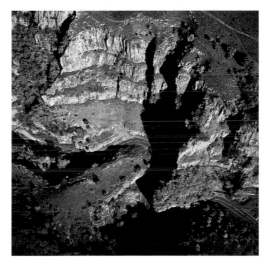

Photography by **ADRIAN WARREN & DAE SASITORN**
Text by **ELIZABETH LOVING & DAVID HALFORD**

LAST REFUGE

For our families

N 56°53'54.1" W 3°12'07.8" Grid Ref: NO269792 Map Ref: 13 H5

The South Esk River in the Grampian Mountains, Scotland

Losgaintir Sands, South Harris, Outer Hebrides
N 57°52'43.3" W 6°56'59.5" Grid Ref: NG067984   Map Ref: 14 D7

CONTENTS

FOREWORD

For such a small island, Britain has a rich and bloody history. People have been living here, on and off, for well over half a million years, and have changed the face of the landscape by cutting forest, digging the land, shaping it, mining its natural resources, and building an ever more complex infrastructure to support a growing and demanding population. One might think that there can be no corners of Britain left to explore, no stones unturned and therefore no more secrets to discover. Yet, each and every year, new evidence comes to light of human interaction with Britain's landscape throughout history, to fill in gradually the gaps in our knowledge.

Some of these discoveries are regularly made through aerial surveys, for the landscape, when viewed from the air, is far more revealing than at ground level. Every time the soil is disturbed, dug or moved, it leaves a mark like a signature. And these marks may still be visible thousands of years later in the form of ghostly lines, odd shapes or colour differences in the soil. They can be subtle, some being quite small marks, while others are more obvious. In places, marks are clustered on top of each other at sites that turned out to be a good strategic choice for a farm, house, or fortification and which was therefore used and re-used through history. Making a flight over Britain is similar to detective work, looking for evidence and trying to unravel its meaning, then matching what is visible in our photographs to previous research by others. Before Neolithic times, however, the people who came here were hunter-gatherers. They led a nomadic lifestyle, leaving very little evidence of their passing, visible either from the air or the ground. But go back even further in time – 3,000 million years ago – and it is possible to trace the geological story of Britain, that is as richly varied as the human story. During that time, the land that would become Britain drifted back and forth across the surface of the earth, accumulating a huge variety of different types of rocks and minerals, making us rich in the resources that would determine our fate.

Over the years since we started flying over Britain for aerial photography, we have become more and more interested in deciphering the landscape to understand its geology and its history, and we are constantly adding new material to our archive. Dipping into this growing resource to select the photographs for this book has not been easy for, inevitably, we have been forced by the restriction of space to leave out many of our favourite shots. At the same time, as the book evolved, we realized how much is still left to do – to photograph locations not yet in our files. As we move forward, we will gradually fill in some of those gaps, with the aid of our trusty Cessna 182.

Adrian Warren & Dae Sasitorn
Somerset, England
September 2007

Mouth of the Great Ouse, near King's Lynn, Norfolk

N 52°48'27.2" E 0°21'22.1" Grid Ref: TF589259 Map Ref: 7 E7

Maiden Castle, Dorset: a massive Iron Age hill fort built over a Neolithic settlement

N 50°41'40.9" W 2°28'11.4"   Grid Ref. SY668885   Map Ref: 3 E8

INTRODUCTION

Britain is Europe's largest island, and the third most populous in the world after Java and Honshu in Japan. Politically it is part of the United Kingdom, which includes Northern Ireland, but Britain itself comprises England, Scotland and Wales together with hundreds of offshore islands such as Orkney and Shetland, the Inner and Outer Hebrides, Isle of Man, Anglesey, Isles of Scilly, Isle of Wight, Lundy and many smaller islands, some little more than rocky outcrops in the sea.

Seen from above, Britain is a patchwork of contrasting landscapes within relatively small distances. Some of these are the consequence of the dramatic forces that have formed the underlying geology, while others result from human influence, and are a living testimony to continuing interaction with the environment over many millennia, in hugely varied climates and sometimes very testing social and political circumstances. The creation of the island of Britain, when the land bridge across the present English Channel disappeared around 7,000 BC, formed a physical barrier that came to have great political, military and psychological significance in the later development of the country.

Around 3,000 BC, a change occurred when nomadic hunter-gatherers became the first farmers. Agriculture enabled people to have a degree of control over their environment and also led to the creation of settled communities. The varied geography of the landscape has contributed to distinct regional identities: life in upland areas required a high degree of innovation and endurance, producing a culture very different from that in places where animal husbandry and crop growing were easier. As numbers of people increased, the management of resources became more and more important, but for centuries agriculture was the mainstay of the economy. The presence of fertile land, mineral resources and plentiful timber attracted settlement, through peaceful migration as well as invasion, and these newcomers – settler and invader alike – helped to shape culture and language. The proximity of the sea created a maritime nation which, especially in the sixteenth and seventeenth centuries, began to look outwards towards the wider world. In common with her European neighbours, Britain acquired an empire; her later dominance of the sea through a powerful navy was an essential factor in maintaining it.

In the nineteenth century, Britain completed the process of industrialization, a process made possible by the availability of mineral resources, especially coal, combined with advances in technology. The effects were profound, changing the landscape and the way in which people lived and worked. For centuries, London has played a special role in the life of the country. First established by the Romans, it was virtually abandoned after their withdrawal. By the mid-eleventh century it was sufficiently important as a centre of wealth and trade for the invading Norman leader, Duke William, to realize that possession of London was an essential element in controlling the country. It later became the centre of government and administration, and was also a focus for internal migration as well as being the first port of call for many newcomers to Britain.

The history of Britain needs to be set in the context of its far longer geological past which has not only influenced its later social and economic development but also provided the stage set against which the human story of the country has been played. Aerial photography provides a unique perspective, giving an insight into how the people of Britain have used and shaped their landscape. The present landscape of the country holds the clues to its past – a story that is both fascinating and complex.

Scotland's Ben Nevis (1343 metres): Britain's highest mountain

N 56°47'54.9" W 5°00'21.3" Grid Ref: NN165715 Map Ref: 12 M5

THE MAKING OF THE LANDSCAPE

Great Britain is the largest island in an archipelago that lies off the north-western coast of the European mainland. It is not a huge landmass – from John O'Groats at the northern tip of Scotland to Land's End in Cornwall is some 1,400 kilometres, and the land area only covers around 240,000 square kilometres – and yet it contains an extraordinary diversity of landscape virtually unequalled anywhere else in the world for a country of its size.

Standing on the limestone pavements at Ingleborough in the Yorkshire Dales, or inside the Iron Age fort on Mam Tor in Derbyshire, it is difficult to imagine them emerging from warm tropical waters akin to the Bahamas. However, these sedimentary rocks contain marine deposits and fossil remains of former tropical reefs and coral atolls south of the equator, formed over 300 million years ago. The cracked and fissured appearance of the pavements is a relatively recent phenomenon, the result of glacial erosion some 10,000 years ago, and subsequent weathering. The majority of Britain's rocks are sedimentary, that is laid down over an extended period, rather than the result of the volcanic activity that created peaks like Snowdon and or the tors of Dartmoor, and so provide a continuous record of British geology.

The geological components of Britain today have been on a lengthy journey, the evidence for which can be traced back over 2,700 million years. Some 750 million years ago the land that was to become this island was located near present-day Antarctica. The map of the world at that time bore no resemblance to that which we see today. The creation of the land masses that form the present world map was endlessly convoluted, with a constant combination and subsequent dispersal of huge land areas. Though the supercontinent of Rodinia is often the starting point for discussing complex geology, this too was the result of three or four continents combining, possibly after an even earlier dispersal. Lying south of the Equator, Rodinia's centre appears to have been Laurentia, the land mass that would eventually form North America, and to the edge of which clung the land that would become Scotland. Geological evidence shows Rodinia breaking up about 800 million years ago amidst extensive volcanic activity. Laurentia in turn spawned Baltica and Amazonia some 600 million years ago, as the Iapetus Ocean opened up.

The origins of what became England and Wales were more recent, as elements of the 'micro-continent' of Avalonia. Some 750 million years ago Avalonia had experienced intense volcanic activity, from which emerged a group of volcanic islands set in shallow seas. Around 550-500 million years ago they appear to have gravitated to the edge of the Gondwana supercontinent. Gondwana broke up to become part of the last of the major supercontinents, Pangaea, in the Silurian period around 440 million years ago, by which time Avalonia had already set off elsewhere on the globe, with the proto-England and Wales grouped in with much of what are now New England, Nova Scotia and Newfoundland, as well as the Low Countries and north-west Germany.

Geographically the oldest rocks in Britain lie to the north and west of the Tees-Exe line, from Northumberland to Devon, and the oldest – the Lewisian gneisses in north-west Scotland and the Outer Hebrides – date from over 2,700 million years ago in the pre-Cambrian period, more than half of all earth's recorded time. These rocks, such as those found beneath Suilven, are Europe's oldest, most of them being igneous – that is volcanic – in origin, with some other elements from later periods. The Scottish Highlands to the east are the result of layers of limestone, sandstone and lava being laid down in the later pre-Cambrian. In fact, Britain is a living textbook for the geologist. During the lower Palaeozoic – the era including the Cambrian (some 570 to 500 million years ago, when the first trilobite fossils appeared), the Ordovician (500 to 440 million years ago) and Silurian periods (440 to 420 million years ago) – and the later Devonian era (its name deriving from red sandstone deposits laid down in Devon some 420 to 350 million years ago, as seen in the formation known as the Old Man of Hoy, Orkney), Britain lay in southern tropical waters. Marine sediments laid down in the Ordivician period in Avalonia can be found in the Skiddaw slates in the Lake District, where volcanic activity is also very visible in the mountains of Scafell Pike and Helvellyn. Fossil-hunters have found remains of complete corals in sites such as the Farley Quarry in Much Wenlock.

Between 444 and 416 million years ago, the two main elements that constitute the British Isles, roughly corresponding to Scotland (attached to Laurentia), and England with Wales (attached to Avalonia), had combined, their impact creating the Caledonian Mountains and those of Western Norway, which originally may have risen to Himalayan heights. The pinky red Ross of Mull granite around the Sound of Iona was formed from molten magma thrust up by the 'collision' around this period, while fields of acid lava spread through Glencoe. Trilobites – marine arthropods – found in fossil form on both sides of the 'join' are very different from each other until after the two land masses joined. These very extensive periods have left traces all over the country, with shales – originally mud from the ocean floors – from the earliest periods, desert sandstones from the Devonian (for example, The Neap in Shetland), and limestones from the Carboniferous (such as those which form the Mendip Hills). Following a gradual northerly track across the Iapetus Ocean, the future Britain reached the equator during the Carboniferous period 300 million years ago. As the mountains slowly eroded, their deposits filtered into the warm shallow seas of the Rheic Ocean, creating huge swamps and rain forests. During this period coal was created from deposits in these areas, with seams running up what would become Britain's east coast, as well as in the Midlands and South Wales. Coal seams can be seen very clearly along the coast between Whitley Bay and Seaton Sluice, while the largest opencast coalmine in Europe is at Stobswood in Northumberland. The Carboniferous footprint can also be seen at places such as the High Force waterfall over Whin Sill, Teesdale, with quartz dolorite, shale and limestone found together, and at Combs Quarry, Ingleborough where it is possible to see Carboniferous limestone sitting directly atop Silurian rocks.

There were further 'collisions' as other elements of Europe combined around the Permian period (around 299 to 251 million years ago), including a period of mountain-building in south-west England that thrust the granite of Dartmoor and Bodmin Moor up through the rock above it. The origins of this granite and that in the Isles of Scilly lie way back in Avalonia's history, in the volcanic activity in the southern hemisphere 700 million years ago. The metamorphic rocks that were created by these same processes were to be the future source of the tin mined extensively in this region. Later weathering also resulted in extensive deposits of kaolin, an essential ingredient of porcelain, but the area was spared the grinding of ice sheets of more recent times, and so has retained its distinctive, rugged feel.

The Permian-Triassic extinction 251.4 million years ago, believed to have been caused by an asteroid hitting earth, led to the death of 96 per cent of marine species and 70 per cent of terrestrial ones. The world took six million years for biodiversity to expand again in the early Triassic period (some 251 to 200 million years ago), when the Zechstein Sea stretched from Britain's east coast to what is now Poland, crossing modern Northern Germany and Denmark. These were periods that saw the creation of the Pennines and Exmoor, with much of Britain turned to desert, creating further sandstones, adding to those of the Devonian period. By the Jurassic (some 200 to 145 million years ago) and Cretaceous periods (around 145 to 4 million years ago) the climate had modified, and the sea increasingly intruded, leaving upland areas as isolated islands. This was the age of dinosaurs, and the most notable remains from this period are the chalk downs and cliffs of southern and eastern England – the eroded remnants of huge mountains. Chalk is a highly frangible material, as demonstrated by the collapsing cliffs at Beachy Head and the chalk stacks of The Needles, off the Isle of Wight. There are huge numbers of fossils of molluscs and sea reptiles in limestone cliffs, such as the ammonites found around Quantoxhead, Somerset, or on the World Heritage Jurassic Coast area of Dorset and Devon near Lyme Regis, along with fossils from the Triassic and Cretaceous. It was also the period when the future wealth of late-twentieth century Britain was laid down, with the burial of algae and zooplankton below the sea floor mud – the organic matter that would result eventually in the creation of North Sea oil and gas deposits. Only by the Lower Tertiary period (around 65 million years ago) would the outline of Britain as it is today begin to emerge, with shallow seas across what is now south-east England created by deposits from huge river systems further north, and the gradual submerging of areas off the west coast. There was also volcanic activity in Scotland, as spectacularly witnessed by the basalt cliffs around Fingal's Cave on Staffa (the result of Lava flows on Mull) and on the north-east coast of Skye. The island of St Kilda was formed from the remains of a partially submerged volcano.

The Atlantic Ocean, so important for Britain's climate, was also beginning to form. On land there were sub tropical swamps, with large mammals including hippopotamus, and mammoth roaming higher ground. This Pleistocene period (about 1.8 million BC to 11,500 BC) also saw the Thames flowing from Wales past Clacton eastwards, as a tributary of the Rhine and later of the English Channel, until the start of the last major ice age. The final remodelling of the British landscape took place during the various ice ages, one of the most severe being about 450,000 years ago, when huge ice caps nearly two kilometres thick spread from the Scottish Highlands to Scandinavia, extending glaciers across lowland Britain, as far south as the River Thames and Bristol Channel. The archetypal glacial valleys and residual moraine deposits from this glaciation, and those of the last Ice Age between 18,000 and 13,000 years ago, and only really ending in Scotland around 8,000 BC, are especially characteristic of much of the Scottish Highlands, and parts of Snowdonia, the Lake District and Yorkshire Dales. Good examples include Lairig Gartain, near the Pass of Glencoe in Scotland and Bannau Sir Gaer, in the Black Mountains of South Wales. The impact of the weight of ice was so severe that the north of Britain has been slowly rising ever since, a phenomenon called 'isostatic rebound', with the earth's outer layer (the lithosphere) springing back up under pressure from the semi-fluid layer below (the asthenosphere). By 6,500 BC this 'isostatic rebound' outran the rising sea levels, with the consequence that many beaches in the north formed during the late-Mesolithic era (around 4,000 BC) had a beach line up to 10 metres above present levels. Meanwhile, southern Britain slowly continues sinking. In the past 800,000 years, nine significant ice ages, with warmer interglacial periods, have affected most parts of Britain. This created an endless cycle of immigration and emigration as early man came and went, following the herds of mammoths, reindeer and other prey northwards across the land bridges that lay across what would become eventually the English Channel and the North Sea.

In case we imagine that our geology has now settled, the earthquake off Folkestone in April 2007, the Carlisle earthquake of 1979, and the regular smaller shocks that emanate from the Severn Valley fault line, act as permanent reminders of the ceaseless activity beneath our feet.

16   Suilven, 731 metres, in north-west Scotland sits on rock over 3 billion years old

Muckle Flugga, Shetland: the northernmost point of Britain, with rock 700 million years old 17

18 Arkle, 787 metres, north-west Scotland: topped by pale Cambrian quartzite, 500 million years old

Ben Nevis, 1343 metres: 400 million years old granite topped by lava

Cairn Toul, 1291 metres, in Scotland's Cairngorms: a granite plateau sculpted by glaciers

Snowdon, 1085 metres, Wales' highest mountain: an extinct volcano eroded by glaciers

22 Cumbria's Scafell Pike, 977 metres: England's highest peak, with volcanic rock 450 million years old

Volcanic cliffs at Eshaness, Shetland, are 400 million years old

The precipitous screes at Wastwater, in Cumbria, are Borrowdale volcanic rock

Newlands Valley, Cumbria, where northern Skiddaw slates meet southern Borrowdale volcanics   25

Devonian red sandstone stacks at the Neap, near Eshaness, Shetland

The Old Man of Hoy, Orkney: a spectacular stack of Devonian red sandstone

28   Bannau Sir Gaer, 749 metres, Black Mountain, Wales: steep flanks scooped out by glaciers

Ingleborough, 724 metres, Yorkshire: Carboniferous limestone pavements exposed by glaciers   29

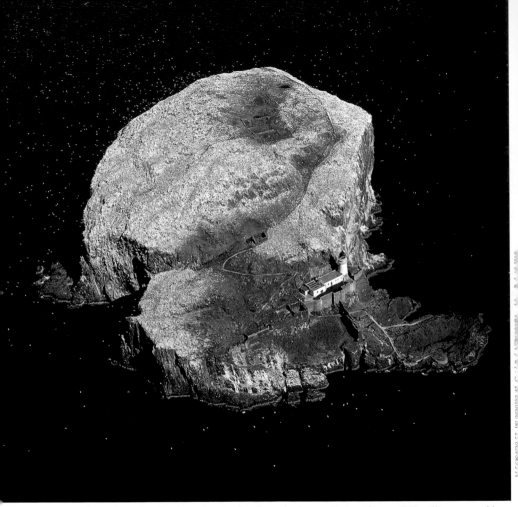

30 Bass Rock, Lothian, Scotland: a volcanic plug from the Lower Carboniferous, 350 million years old

Haytor Rocks, Dartmoor, Devon: granite from the late Carboniferous, 280 million years old 31

32   Dyer's Lookout, near Hartland Point, Devon: folding of Carboniferous rocks 300 million years old

Salcombe Hill Cliff, near Sidmouth, Devon: 250 million years old Triassic Mercia Mudstone cliff 33

34   Gad Cliff, Brandy Bay, Dorset: limestone, chalk and sandstone from the Jurassic, rich in fossils

Continually collapsing cliffs at Cain's Folly, Charmouth, Dorset, expose fossils from the Jurassic period **35**

36   Cliffs east of Kimmeridge Ledges, Dorset: Upper Jurassic clay, a source rock for oil

Buckton Cliffs, near Flamborough, Yorkshire: chalks and clays from Cretaceous and Jurassic periods

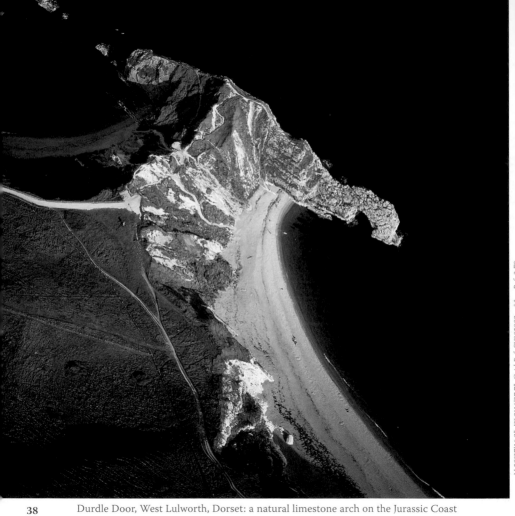

Durdle Door, West Lulworth, Dorset: a natural limestone arch on the Jurassic Coast

Old Harry Rocks, near Swanage, Dorset: chalk stacks formed by erosion on the Jurassic Coast

40 The Needles, Isle of Wight: chalk cliffs eroding to form pointed stacks due to almost vertical strata

Beachy Head, Sussex: continually collapsing chalk cliffs from the Cretaceous, 90 million years ago **41**

Ardnamurchan volcanic crater, Western Highlands, Scotland: active 60 million years ago

Hirta, St Kilda, the westernmost island archipelago of Scotland: an extinct volcano 60 million years old **43**

44   Kilt Rock waterfall, Isle of Skye: 65 metres high, it plunges over cliffs of basalt to the sea below

Fingal's Cave on the island of Staffa, Inner Hebrides: the cliffs of basalt are 60 million years old   **45**

46   Loch Ness and the Great Glen: a huge geological fault that effectively splits Scotland into two

Salcombe, Devon: sited in a drowned river valley formed as south-west England sinks into the sea 47

48 Brimham Rocks, North Yorkshire: millstone grit 320 million years old has weathered into bizarre shape

Bedshiel, Borders, Scotland: a ridge of sand deposited by a river flowing within a melting glacier **49**

Lairig Gartain, near Glencoe, Scotland: a glacial valley

Glen Titl, Cairngorms, Scotland: a classic U-shaped glacial valley

52 Coniston Water, Cumbria: Ice Age glaciers scooped out soft rock to form a long valley that later flooded

Little Loch Broom, north-west Highlands of Scotland: a glacial trough partly flooded by the sea **53**

54 Gordale Scar, Yorkshire: carved as a rock tunnel by meltwater under an ice-sheet, until the roof collaps[e]

Wharfdale, North Yorkshire: Kettlewell nestles in a valley formed by a glacier

56 Alport Dale, Derbyshire: the Peak District plateau has been deeply incised by the action of water

Lulworth Cove, Dorset: the sea breached outer defences of Portland stone to create a natural harbour   57

St Ninian's tombolo, Shetland: a sandbar connects the island to the mainland

Wicken Fen, Cambridgeshire: the low-lying fens were saltmarsh until reclaimed by drainage 59

Chesil Beach, Dorset: a storm shingle beach, at 29 km, the longest tombolo in Britain

Orford Beach, Suffolk: a natural spit of sand and shingle that protects the coast from the North Sea **61**

62   Lynmouth, Devon: flash floods on the River Lyn have deposited vast silt banks at the estuary

Barrisdale Bay, in Scotland's Loch Hourn: a fjord-like sea loch carved by glaciation

The Wash at Clay Hole: man-made channels help to drain the Fens

Keyhaven Saltmarsh, Hampshire, an ecologically rich area at the western end of the Solent

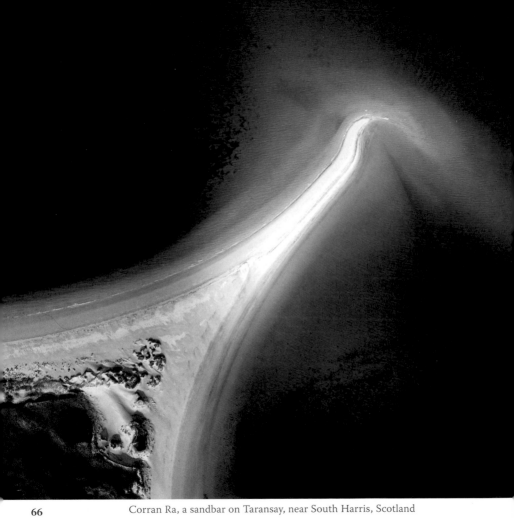

Corran Ra, a sandbar on Taransay, near South Harris, Scotland

Colli Ness, Sanday Island, Orkney: possibly inundated by the sea until recent times

Samson and Tresco, the Scilly Isles: a lump of granite gradually sinking into the sea

Knock and Lochan topography near Suilven, north-west Highlands, Scotland: a post-glacial landscape **69**

Forest canopy at Creswell, Derbyshire: much of Britain was once forest-covered

The Forest of Dean, Gloucestershire, includes over 100 square km of ancient mixed woodland

Meanders on the River Earn, near Perth, as it flows across the flood plain to meet the River Tay

Afon Dwyryd River, upstream from Portmeirion, in Gwynedd, North Wales

Cheddar Gorge, Somerset: inhabited by cave dwelling people 13,000 years ago

FROM STONE TO BRONZE
Prehistory – 800 BC

Our earliest ancestors came out of Africa – *Homo erectus*, whose first recorded remains in Africa date from around 1.8 million years ago, and *Homo habilis*. During much of the Pleistocene era in Britain (from around 1,808,000 BC to 11,500 BC), there was a regular pattern of settlement and departure in line with climate changes, and it has not always been possible to establish when Britain was connected to mainland Europe.

At Pakefield near Lowestoft, the discovery of flint tools – for butchering the mammoths whose remains were found at the site – has recently established the earliest known human occupation in Northern Europe, dating to approximately 700,000 BC. No human remains from this period have yet been discovered, but the tools must have been produced by an ancestor of early man (*Homo heidelbergensis*), who first appeared in Europe around 800,000 BC. He had a medium-sized brain, but the massive brow and lack of chin characteristic of primitive man. Previous research had first placed early man in Britain 550,000 years ago at Happisburgh on the crumbling Norfolk coast, and at the site of Boxgrove, Sussex, dating from 500,000 BC, where the remains of a tibia of a powerfully built man of 1.8 metres were discovered in 1993. Thousands of artefacts, including well-made flint axes and scrapers, were found alongside horse remains. He was part of a group, so collaborative hunting was clearly being practised some 200,000 years ahead of the advent of Neanderthal Man. Contemporary population numbers were very small, possibly around 5,500.

The period known as the Anglian glacial began around 450,000 BC, wiping out most British fauna. A chalk land bridge from Dover to Calais had held back waters in the North Sea and Rhine, creating a huge lake, but eventually this dam broke, scouring out the English Channel. From then on, Britain was cut off from the mainland, except during the various ice ages, when the ice sheets retained vast quantities of water. The Anglian glacial lasted 50,000 years, after which ice returned. Fossilised skull fragments 250,000 years old of a pre-Neanderthal woman were found at Swanscombe in Kent, at a site especially rich in hand axes. Estimates of population size in the middle Palaeolithic (350,000 to 33,000 BC) are 10,000 to 27,000 throughout the British Isles. Around 125,000 BC there was a very warm spell, the Ipswichian interglacial, with hippos basking where Trafalgar Square now stands, yet no human presence at that time can be established.

The Neanderthals reached Britain around 200,000 years ago, perhaps as an evolved descendant of *H. heidelbergensis*. Their most northerly remains found to date, an adult and two children, were discovered in Pontnewydd Cave in North Wales, together with hand axes and spear tips. By 30,000 BC they disappear from the human record, but how or why is unknown. There appears to have been no intermarriage with modern man (*Homo sapiens*). Their remains suggest that Neanderthal males were around 1.7 metres tall, with powerful bodies, and a maximum lifespan of 40 years.

The so-called 'Red Lady' of Goat's Hole Cave, Paviland, Gower was not, as first thought, a woman from the Roman period but a male from 26,000 years ago. He and his ancestors had arrived in Britain 10,000 years earlier, yet this man's DNA is very similar to modern man. His was a ritual burial, with ivory artefacts and red ochre powder, implying a belief system of some sort. The cave is now on the Welsh foreshore, but then would have been 100 kilometres from the sea above a game-rich plain, with water trapped in ice sheets further north.

The harsh climate ensured an intermittent human presence. The last thaw started around 13,000 years ago and in Gough's Cave in the Cheddar Gorge, a human group from about 12,000 BC was found, their bodies dismembered like the horses, red deer and reindeer they ate. Was this a ritual killing or cannibalism? In 2003, about 80 low-relief figures of animals were found on the walls of Church Hole cave at Cresswell Crags, dating from the same period. There was also a revolution in hunting technology at this time with the appearance of the bow and arrow. The North Sea area was still passable in 10,000 BC and was initially tundra roamed by reindeer and horses, with deer and pigs appearing as the climate got warmer. Artefacts have been found 40 kilometres off the Norfolk coast, at a depth of some 40 metres – the inhabitants of Starr Carr could have walked to Holland. By 6,000 BC the area was once again covered by water, as the North Sea rose by 130 metres.

The chance sight of a lobster scrabbling on the seabed off the Isle of Wight, surrounded by flint knives and scrapers, led to the discovery of one of the most interesting recent finds in Britain – a settlement from the Mesolithic period that had sat on top of the now sunken Bouldnor Cliff in the Solent for more than 8,000 years. (The Mesolithic covers the Middle Stone Age from about 8,500 BC to 4,000 BC.) The loss of coastal sites as waters rose may explain why we have scant hard evidence on Mesolithic humans. What little we know is largely derived from the variety of stone and flint tools that they fashioned. The traditional view was of groups of hunter-gatherers foraging widely for food, the rhythm of their lives dictated by the flow of the seasons, sourcing from whatever they could kill or pick. Recent research however has discovered that, from the mid-Mesolithic, there was significant continuing use of land in some areas such as the Tyne Valley, and Scottish island sites such as Islay and Colonsay.

Pollen samples from cereals indicate early attempts at crop growing, as well as the processing and storage of nuts and tubers, evidence for which goes back 10,500 years at Cramond on the Firth of Forth. Habitation sites in England include Howick in Northumberland – where a posthole circle and detritus revealed Britain's oldest known house dating from around 7,800 BC. Britain's most important Mesolithic site, Starr Carr near Pickering, first occupied around 8,700 BC, was a regular but seasonal hunting camp. Research on vegetation types show relatively open areas, with birch and pine trees not dissimilar to parts of Scandinavia today being gradually replaced by mixed deciduous forest as post-ice age temperatures rose, inhibiting travel and hunting. This led to greater clearance of forest and woodlands than was previously thought. Fire was the primary agent, either to drive prey towards the hunters, or to create clearings where animals might collect and be killed.

Information about the Mesolithic and later periods are frustratingly elusive. There are no remains of boats in Britain to explain how offshore islands were reached, but elsewhere in Europe there is evidence of large canoes. Many bone engravings and stone carvings have been found in mainland Europe, but they are almost totally absent from British sites. Population figures are highly speculative, possibly between 10,000 and 30,000.

Negotiating the narrow split trunks of the two-kilometre long 'Sweet Track' across the Somerset Levels in 3,806 BC could have been a dangerous business. Built by placing narrow split oak trunks in the 'V' of crossed poles driven into the mud, it was part of a wide network of Neolithic pathways across the marshes extending further than we see today. Dendrochronology (the science of dating from tree rings) enables the Sweet Track to be dated very accurately, making these the oldest timber tracks discovered in Northern Europe. From the Neolithic period (around 4,000 to 2,200 BC) early society begins to come more into focus. It was a significant period of change, possibly with some migration from mainland Europe, but less so than once thought. The population expanded slowly, initially still roaming like its Mesolithic ancestors, but livestock, not just game, would provide an increasing amount of food, along with wheat that was beginning to be cultivated more extensively. Pottery with distinctive patterning also began to appear, along with more sophisticated tools such as flint leaf-shaped arrowheads, and stone axes. In the mid-Neolithic period (from around 3,000 BC) the hunter-gatherer became a farmer, with a stake in the land that he had cleared and sown, and ownership of the animals that supplied his food. Native species and varieties would be supplemented by introduced ones, such as barley, as well as sheep and goats, a major source of protein and clothing.

The first evidence for religious observances appeared in the early-Neolithic (around 3,500 BC) in the form of barrows for burials and 'cursus' monuments, as well as ritual enclosures in the mid- to late-Neolithic. By around 2,500 BC, the first stones had been raised within Stonehenge's earth ramparts, created some 900 years earlier on Salisbury Plain. Wood was also widely used, such as at Woodhenge and Norfolk's Seahenge. Excavations at the large 500-metre diameter henge at Durrington Walls, which had been built three kilometres away from Stonehenge, have revealed eight buildings and two timber post circles inside the earthworks. The great stone circle at Avebury, 35 kilometres to the north, is more accurately named a 'henge' than its neighbour, as the impressive 1.35 kilometre ditch is inside the earthen ramparts rather than outside. It encloses two stone circles, each some 100 metres in diameter, the southern one partly buried beneath the village, with the West Kennet Avenue of standing stones running up to the south-east corner. Outside the site are three important further monuments, including the largest prehistoric man-made mound in Europe, Silbury Hill, a 40-metre high artificial mound covering two hectares and dating from about 2,600 BC, the West Kennet Long Barrow and the Sanctuary.

North of Ripon in Yorkshire lies one of the least known Neolithic landscapes in Britain, the Thornborough Henges. Contemporary with Stonehenge, three 240-metre diameter henge circles stand in an almost straight line, each linked by avenues of 550 metres with the whole stretching approximately two kilometres. Of the three, the tree-covered northern henge is the best preserved. A cursus, a long and narrow rectangular area enclosed by a bank and surrounded by a ditch, runs through the central henge, supposedly pointing at the constellation Orion. Britain's largest cursus is the Dorset Cursus on Cranborne Chase. Dating from between 2,800-2,200 BC, it is 10 kilometres long and 100 metres wide, and runs across several valleys.

The most remote Neolithic landscape in Britain is found on Orkney. The nine-metre long passageway into the great corbelled central chamber of Maes Howe, built around 2,800 BC on the main island of the Orkney archipelago, is orientated to catch the sun's rays at the winter solstice. It is now the focus of a World Heritage site that includes two nearby stone circles – the Stones of Stenness and the Ring of Brodgar. Maes Howe's purpose is unclear, but is assumed to have been a burial site, abandoned around 2,000 BC as the climate worsened. Most impressive is the nearby Ring of Brodgar, where 27 of the original 60 stones stand in a ring 104 metres in diameter, surrounded by a rock-cut ditch. This outstanding Neolithic landscape is further distinguished by the presence of Skara Brae, Europe's best preserved Neolithic village, a complex of eight houses on the west coast of Orkney. Occupied from about 3,100 BC to 2,500 BC, it owes its insulation and preservation to being built into a midden. The remains give a vivid idea of living conditions, each house with a fireplace, stone shelves, seats and drains for primitive toilets. At that time, Britain's total population may have numbered only around 250,000.

The spread of the 'beaker' culture from Holland and the Rhineland to Britain first introduced metallurgical skills to Britain. The constituents of bronze, chosen for its workability and durability, were found in the copper mines of Wales and the tin mines of Devon and Cornwall: the combination of eight parts copper to one part tin produced bronze. Wales has the largest Bronze Age copper mine in the world, at Great Orme's Head near Llandudno, dating from around 1,600 BC to 1,200 BC, with some 15 kilometres of shafts and tunnels, giving an extraordinary insight into prehistoric industry. Some tunnels are barely 50 centimetres across, implying the presence of women and children in the workforce, all working with primitive axes and antler scrapers. In Devon and Cornwall by contrast, Roman and later workings have erased any trace of the Bronze Age tin mining that had started around the same time as the Welsh copper mine.

There is still uncertainty over whether the influence in Britain of the 'beaker peoples' was from migration, and possibly invasion, around 1,200 BC, or from the adoption of an imported cultural knowledge 'package', affecting everything from technological skills to religious observances. The inverted bell-shaped 'beaker' pottery imported from the continent was only one item in an increasing trading relationship with mainland Europe. Cornish tin was exported to Ireland and the continent, and reached the Mediterranean by way of Phoenician traders in the late Bronze Age.

Farming began to impose recognisable structures that have in some cases survived today as field patterns, and which are particularly striking from the air. On Dartmoor there is evidence of co-axial field patterns – strictly symmetrical fields between lines of parallel walls. There is also Dunnabridge Pound, a large enclosure for illegally pastured animals, with origins in the Bronze Age. Fragments of Bronze Age field patterns remain in Wiltshire, such as at Burderop Down, but as with so many other sites around the country, most has been erased by intensive farming over the centuries.

Some routes around Britain used by Bronze Age man are still visible, and indeed the Tarr Steps on Exmoor are a classic clapper bridge constructed from stone slabs around 1,000 BC. The Ridgeway, the great Neolithic trunk route that originally ran across southern England from the Wash to Dorset, follows high ground past numerous prehistoric sites, but now finishes near Avebury. It passes some of the great chalk figures so characteristic of southern Britain, such as the White Horse of Uffington, dating from about 1,000 BC.

One of the finest late Bronze Age sites is to be found at Flag Fen, near Peterborough, where a timber platform was built at the mouth of a bay as seawater flooded the fens. It was linked to the shore by a line of posts nearly one kilometre long. Hundreds of bronze and tin artefacts from the Bronze and Iron Ages, including rings, swords and spears, were found along its length. The practice of burying bodies or ashes was gradually giving way to depositions in watery places, whose sacred nature became increasingly important to later Iron Age man.

By about 900 BC, the intensity of farming had already turned the New Forest and much of South Dorset into unproductive heathlands. Farmers made increasing use of sheep and their wool as textiles became more sophisticated. Granaries were constructed for storage, and the development of the salt industry ensured that meat could be preserved and transported. Perhaps most importantly, the wheel made its first appearance. The boundary between the Bronze and Iron Ages becomes blurred, as there are characteristics of each period in the other, but the ability to work with iron, and to transport heavy goods in wheeled carts, was to be an important step forward as Britain put the Neolithic world firmly behind it.

Happisburgh, Norfolk, where coastal erosion by the North Sea exposed palaeolithic flint tools **79**

Boxgrove, West Sussex: work in a gravel pit revealed a 500,000 years old human bone

Swanscombe, Kent, where 400,000 years old hand axes were discovered

82 Cliffs at Paviland, Gower, South Wales, where a 29,000 year old human skeleton was found in a cave

Creswell Crags, Derbyshire: the only known site in Britain for Palaeolithic cave art, 15,000 years old **83**

84   Star Carr, Yorkshire: site of a Mesolithic hunting camp, 10,700 years ago

Somerset Levels, where peat workings revealed the Sweet Track, a walkway built 5,800 years ago **85**

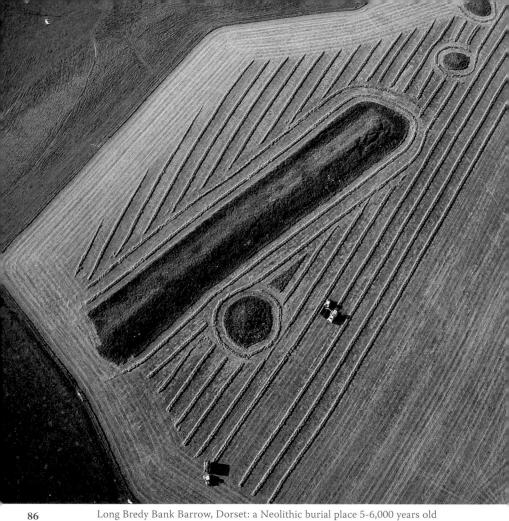

Long Bredy Bank Barrow, Dorset: a Neolithic burial place 5-6,000 years old

West Kennet Long Barrow, Wiltshire: a Neolithic chambered barrow 5,600 years old   87

Silbury Hill, Wiltshire: the tallest man-made mound in Europe, built 4,750 years ago

Avebury, Wiltshire: a Neolithic henge 5,000 years old containing the largest known stone circle **89**

Worbarrow, Dorset: an excavated Neolithic long barrow 5,500 years old

Castlerigg Stone Circle, Cumbria: a Neolithic stone circle 5,000 years old

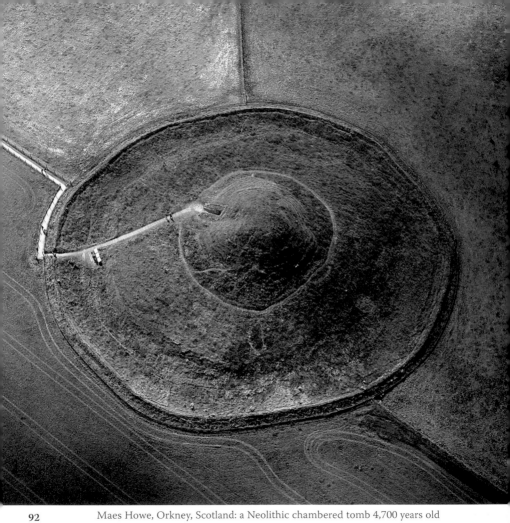

Maes Howe, Orkney, Scotland: a Neolithic chambered tomb 4,700 years old

Skara Brae, Orkney, Scotland: a Neolithic village with stone-built houses occupied 5,100 years ago **93**

94   Grimes Graves, Norfolk: a massive Neolithic flint mine 5,000 years old with over 400 shafts

Standing Stones of Stenness, Orkney, Scotland: a Neolithic ritual site built 5,000 years ago

Thornborough Henges, North Yorkshire: a ritual landscape 5,000 years old

The Ring of Brodgar, Stenness, Orkney: a stone circle 4,500 years old

98 Maumbury Rings, Dorchester, Dorset: a Neolithic henge later adapted as a Roman amphitheatre

Knowlton Henge, Dorset: part of a Neolithic ritual complex

Stonehenge, Wiltshire: a remarkable ritual site over 5,000 years old

Priddy Circles, Somerset: Neolithic henges over 4,000 years old

Windmill Hill, Wiltshire: a Neolithic causewayed enclosure

Rybury Camp, Wiltshire: a Neolithic causewayed enclosure

The Sanctuary Stone Circle: part of the Avebury ritual complex, Wiltshire

Arbor Low, Derbyshire: a Neolithic henge 4,500 years old

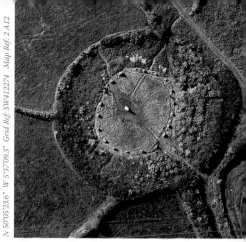

N 50°05'23.6" W 5°37'09.3" Grid Ref: SW412274 Map Ref: 2 A12

Boscawen-Un: a Bronze Age stone circle, Cornwall

Tregeseal East: a Bronze Age stone circle, Cornwall

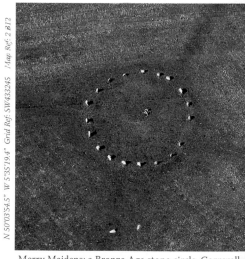

N 50°03'54.5" W 5°35'19.4" Grid Ref: SW433245 Map Ref: 2 B12

Merry Maidens: a Bronze Age stone circle, Cornwall

106   Callanish Stone Circle, Lewis, Scotland: a Neolithic ritual site almost 5,000 years old

Torhouse Stone Circle, Dumfries and Galloway, Scotland

108 Devil's Humps, Bow Hill barrow cemetery, West Sussex: Bronze Age bowl barrows 3,700 years old

Upwey Disc Barrow, Ridgeway, Dorset: an enormous Bronze Age disc barrow 3,700 years old   **109**

Poor Lot Barrows, Dorset: Bronze Age burial site 3,700 years old

Oakley Down Barrows, Dorset: Bronze Age burial site 3,700 years old

Grimspound Bronze Age Settlement, Dartmoor, Devon

Bronze Age fields near Lower Cator, Dartmoor

Hambledon Hill: an Iron Age hill fort and Neolithic causewayed enclosure, Dorset

Eildon Hill North, near Melrose, Borders, Scotland: a Bronze Age hill fort

116 Uffington White Horse, Oxfordshire: a Bronze Age hill figure thought to date from around 1,000 BC

Foales Arrishes Bronze Age and Iron Age settlement, Dartmoor, Devon

Dunnabridge Pound, Dartmoor: a large enclosure for animals, with Bronze Age origins

Part of the world largest known Bronze Age copper mine at Great Orme, Llandudno, North Wales **119**

Maiden Castle, Dorset: a massive Iron Age hill fort built over a Neolithic settlement

THE IRON AGE

800 BC – AD 43

'alkers in the woods of the Weald in East Sussex may barely glance at the occasional small pond, yet some are iron ore ts – the forgotten vestiges of a time nearly 2,500 years ago when the extraction and working of iron first took hold in is area. Iron, the metal that defined the age, as bronze had the previous era, was gradually introduced throughout the untry, starting in the southern lowlands. Iron ore was more widely available than copper and tin, and did not need y alloy process. More than a hundred extraction sites have been identified in the Weald – from the Anglo-Saxon ord for 'forest' – which was a major source of quality ore and had limitless supplies of wood for charcoal.

he technique for working iron had developed possibly as early as 2,000 BC. There is evidence to suggest that it was own in India around this time, but certainly iron weapons were being made in Anatolia from around 1,500 BC d the technology reached Britain during the first millennium BC. Although iron tools were being made during the ghth century BC, the use of iron did not become widespread until some four hundred years later. It was smelted ing the 'bloomery' method, where alternating layers of ore and charcoal were built up and then lit before being vered in clay to create a type of oven. Bellows fanned the flames, but primitive furnaces like this were incapable of aching a temperature high enough to produce iron without impurities, and so the resultant iron ball was hammered or wrought – into shape. The implication of this technology was profound, particularly in agriculture which was volutionized by the iron-tipped plough.

e owe our earliest information on Iron Age Britain to a Greek, Pytheas of Massilia (modern Marseilles), who sailed Britain between 330 BC and 320 BC as part of a longer voyage to the Arctic and the Baltic. What he called the island Albion was inhabited by people calling themselves 'Pretani' – the origin of the Roman name 'Britannia'. Albion as not a remote archipelago but a country very much on the tin trade map for Phoenicians from at least the eighth ntury BC, and supported a population that, just before the Roman invasion, may have been as high as three million. 445 BC, the Greek historian Herodotus referred to the British Isles as the Tin Islands or 'Cassiterides'. Whether not the people of Britain can be described as Celts is much contested, but most scholars now agree that, while ere were linguistic, social and cultural similarities, there was no over-arching pan-European, homogeneous 'Celtic' lture, and that the term 'Celtic' should be used sparingly, and mainly in the context of language.

cept in those areas that were largely ignored by the Roman invaders, such as Cornwall, the generally accepted period the Iron Age in Britain is from about 700 BC to the Roman invasion under Emperor Claudius in AD 43. It was a riod of change in activities such as agriculture, as forests were cleared and the iron-tipped plough, increasingly used the climate turned wetter, proved far more effective at turning over the heavy clay soils. Yields of wheat, barley, and estock increased, while pulses, flax and other crops were farmed more widely. This agricultural prosperity, especially eat, would have been one of Britain's attractions to later Roman invaders. Traces of prehistoric field systems can ll be found at places such as Fengate near Peterborough, at Fyfield Down on Salisbury Plain, Smacam Down and atton Down in Dorset, and in the Yorkshire Dales, with extensive remains in Malhamdale and in Wharfedale. ere 'co-axial' or parallel field boundaries – earth or stone banks – run like a ladder laid across the landscape. Similar tterns are to be found on the Waveney floodplain in Suffolk and elsewhere. More than three thousand Iron Age sites in Britain are still visible, while outlines of at least another three thousand can also be identified from the air through crop marks.

Julius Caesar has left a description of Britons in the mid-first century BC in his account of the Gallic Wars. He describes their multicoloured shirts and striped or checked coats, secured by shoulder buckles, with some men wearing large embossed helmets, and their practice of dying themselves blue with woad before battle. There were no cities, and communities lived on farms or at best in large villages. Families mostly lived in single-roomed roundhouses built of timber posts, with perhaps an area screened off, the walls sealed with wattle and daub (clay mixed with straw, applied over interwoven willow or hazel branches) with some form of thatched roof.

Foel Drygard, at the edge of the Preseli Mountains in Wales, has at least 220 identifiable roundhouse platforms from different periods. Mostly only the postholes and foundations, storage holes and drainage channels are visible today. Sites such as the late Iron Age stone-built village of Chysauster near Penzance, with its multi-roomed courtyard houses, are relatively rare. However, replica roundhouses have been built at Castell Henllys in Wales and Butser Farm in Hampshire, which give a vivid sense of the period. The roundhouse was continued in stone in northern and western Scotland, and elsewhere if wood was scarce, with the style evolving into 'Atlantic roundhouses' and later in some cases, into the tall, conical, double-walled, multi-roomed brochs whose remains still dominate parts of the Hebrides (Dun Carloway and Loch na Berie), Orkney (Gurness and Midhowe) and the Shetland Isles, with its wheelhouses and multi-layered Jarlshof site. Mousa on Shetland is the most complete example.

The outstanding monuments from the Iron Age are the great hill forts that even now, some 2,500 years after they were built, impress with their scale and complexity. Some like Ladle Hill and Chanctonbury Ring are simple circles enclosed by a single rampart and ditch. Others such as Maiden Castle, the largest multivallate one in Britain with its origins in Neolithic times, are elliptical, with multiple ramparts and complex, multi-layered access routes. Here ramparts still stand six metres high. They would have been crowned with wooden palisades, presenting a formidable barrier to all but the most determined attacker. Unfortunately the Roman general – and later Emperor – Vespasian was one of those, and numerous artefacts from the second legion's successful attack in AD 43 have been found. Many forts – such as Mount Caburn, Danebury, Badbury Rings, Eggardon and Herefordshire Beacon – are spread across southern England, but numerous others stretch across central England and Wales, from Uffington Castle, Caer Caradoc, and Old Oswestry to Moel Arthur, Carn Fadryn and Caer Penrhos. Scotland is well represented too at sites such as Eildon Hill North, White Caterthun, Traprain Law and Corsehope Rings. A further peculiarity in Scotland are the vitrified forts, some 50 in all, where intense heat, possibly produced during their destruction by fire, has turned stone walls into a glasslike substance. A striking example is Tap O'Noth in Aberdeenshire. The location of some hill forts seems to indicate that permanent occupation and defence were not always the primary purposes. And not all forts were on hills. Excavations at Stanwick near Richmond, Yorkshire have shown it to be the site of the biggest Iron Age fort in Britain, with more than nine kilometres of ditches and ramparts. The lake villages on the Somerset Levels at Glastonbury and Mere also reveal another form of protection – inaccessibility – and were used probably only in summer months. A further development, but whether for defence or storage is unclear, were the underground, stone-lined tunnels (souterrains) found widely in Scotland – such as at Pitcur and Castlelaw – and in England, especially in Cornwall (where they are known as 'fogous'), at sites such as Carn Euny and Pendeen. There are also linear structures such as Grim's Ditch (or Grim's Dyke), bank and ditch earthworks possibly dating from round 300 BC, or from the eighth and ninth centuries in Saxon times. This follows part of the ancient track of the Ridgeway through southern Oxfordshire. It is hard to assess its original purpose from its current height, and it may have simply been a territorial boundary.

Julius Caesar also provides a vivid portrait of the Druids, the priestly caste exempt from military service and tribute, who acted as judges in disputes, and as a source of instruction to many young men. He describes their human sacrifices, designed to improve fortunes of war and to mitigate outbreaks of disease. There are relatively few surviving Iron Age temple sites, as many were transformed later by the Romans, but on Hayling Island there are traces of a circular shrine surrounded by rectangular enclosures, where numerous votive offerings were found.

Many artefacts have been found in rivers or other watery sites, probably offerings reflecting the importance of water in contemporary beliefs that dated back to the Bronze Age or earlier. Graves have also been a rich source of artefacts in those communities where elaborate burials, with the deceased's possessions, were the custom. In East Yorkshire there are a series of 'square barrows', circular mounds surrounded by a square ditch, the largest being about 16 metres across. These contained personal items including weapons, and occasionally two-wheeled carts or chariots, a tradition that echoes contemporary continental practice. It was here that the 'Kirkburn sword', dating from between 300 and 200 BC and described by the British Museum as probably the finest in Europe, was found in 1987. However, most people do not appear to have made such elaborate arrangements, and so relatively few sites are known. The large number of artefacts found in water suggest that many dead were probably disposed of in rivers and lakes.

One of the finest treasure hoards was found at Snettisham in Norfolk. It includes 75 complete bronze, gold and silver torques, and coins found alongside suggest they were buried around 70 BC, yet there is no sign of any Iron Age settlement nearby. Airfield building work on the island of Anglesey in the Second World War revealed the Llyn Cerrig Bach treasure, 150 bronze and iron objects, including swords, shields, spears, chariot wheels and cauldrons that had been preserved in peat from a former lake. Anglesey was the centre of Druidic culture, and the lake could have been a focus for their rituals. Less glamorous but no less important are the finds from middens, the rubbish heaps of a community, which have produced examples of pots, some still with food attached, and animal bones that indicate the nature of local diet. Some remains found within or close to settlements were deliberately buried for ritual purposes, including complete animal carcasses and human bones. Some finds can be gruesome. The Lindow Man's perfectly preserved body was found in a peat bog in Cheshire, and it was clear that he had been sacrificed, his head battered and his throat cut. Though much of the population was engaged in agriculture, there were also centres of industrial activity round the country, with salt workings in the western part of Chichester Harbour, protected by Tourner Bury Hill Fort, as well as in the Welland Valley north of Peterborough. Iron ore was extracted from numerous sites, from bowl-shaped opencast pits measuring up to 18 metres wide and 14 deep.

With scant documentary sources, it is difficult to find named individuals emerging from the shadows, but some hints are provided by the coinage, as British tribal leaders put their names on coins produced from the late first century BC. The Silsden Hoard contained 27 gold coins minted by Cunebolinus, who comes down to us through history as Shakespeare's 'Cymbeline'. He seems to have come to power in St Albans in AD 9, maintained good relations with Rome, and was succeeded by his son Caratacus around AD 35. In 2002, several thousand gold and silver coins were found in Leicestershire, not an area that had previously attracted much research. There is clearly a great deal more Iron Age history still to be excavated from digs before anything like a full picture emerges.

Mam Tor Hill Fort, Derbyshire

Clovelly Dykes, Devon: an Iron Age hill fort with outer enclosures for animal stock

Hod Hill, Dorset: Roman fort built within an Iron Age hill fort

Michael's Mount, Cornwall: an Iron Age trading centre for visiting ships seeking tin and other goods **127**

128   Wandlebury Hill Fort, in the Gog Magog Hills, Cambridgeshire: built some 2,500 years ago

Meggs Hill, in the Gog Magog Hills, Cambridgeshire

Abbotsbury Castle Hill Fort, Dorset

N 50°40'37.9" W 2°37'47.7" Grid Ref: SY556866 Map Ref: 3 D8

Chalbury Ring Hill Fort, Dorset

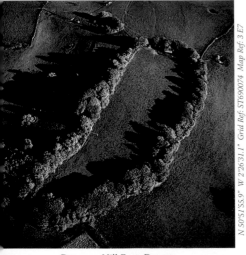

N 50°51'55.9" W 2°26'31.1" Grid Ref: ST690074 Map Ref: 3 E7

Dungeon Hill Fort, Dorset

Coney's Castle Hill Fort, Dorset

Badbury Rings, Dorset: an early Iron Age hill fort about 2,800 years old

Tre'r Ceiri Hill Fort, near Nefyn, Gwynedd, North Wales, is about 2,000 years old

Pen-y-Cloddiau Hill Fort, Flintshire, North Wales

N 53°12'22.1" W 3°5'22.6" Grid Ref: SH750693 Map Ref: 8 E11

Pen-y-Gaer Hill Fort, Conwy, North Wales

Penrhos Hill Fort & 12th century castle, Ceredigion, Wales

N 52°42'48.5" W 3°01'45.5" Grid Ref: SJ306.134 Map Ref: 6 A4

Middletown Hill Fort, The Breidden, Powys, Wales

Moel Arthur Hill Fort, Denbighshire, Wales

Carn Fadryn Hill Fort, on the Llyn Peninsula, Gwynedd, North Wales

136 Cissbury Ring, near Worthing, West Sussex: an Iron Age hill fort and Neolithic flint mines

Chanctonbury Ring, West Sussex: an Iron Age hill fort, about 2,400 years old

Beacon Hill Fort, Hampshire: an Iron Age hill fort, about 2,200 years old

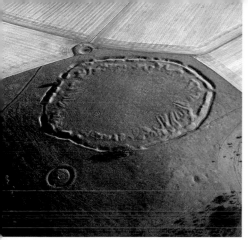

Ladle Hill, Hampshire: hill fort that was never finished

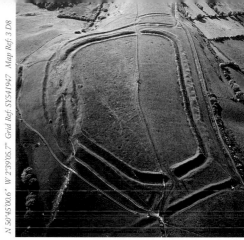

N 50°45'00.6" W 2°39'05.7" Grid Ref: SY541947 Map Ref: 3 D8

Eggardon Hill, Dorset

Pilsdon Pen Hill Fort, Dorset

N 50°53'33.3" W 0°45'13.8" Grid Ref: SU877:11 Map Ref: 4 A10

The Trundle, St Roche's Hill, West Sussex

140 British Camp, an Iron Age hill fort on Herefordshire Beacon in the Malvern Hills, Worcestershire

Tap O'Noth vitrified Hill Fort, Aberdeenshire, Scotland

White Cathertun Hill Fort, Angus, Scotland

Oswestry Hill Fort, Shropshire: dates back some 2,600 years

144 Carn Euny, Cornwall: an Iron Age village with a fogou, was still occupied during the Roman perio

Chysauster, Cornwall: an Iron Age and Romano-British village

Broch of Gurness, on Mainland Orkney: an Iron Age tower built some 2,200 years ago

Midhowe Broch, on Rousay, Orkney: occupied for some 400 years from about 2,200 years ago

Mousa Broch, Shetland: the best preserved example of an Iron Age tower

Clickhimin Broch, near Lerwick, Shetland, Scotland

149

Dun Carloway Broch, Isle of Lewis, Scotland

Stanwick Camp, North Yorkshire: a late Iron Age hill fort enclosing some 750 acres of land

152   Iron Age and Romano-British field systems on Fyfield Down, near Avebury, Wiltshire

Iron Age fields and Romano-British settlement at Smacam Down, Dorset

Hadrian's Wall and Milecastle 37, near Housesteads, Northumberland, looking west

ROMAN BRITAIN

AD 43 – 410

Their home city of Hama, on the River Orontes in modern Syria, must have seemed very far away to the archers in the second century AD who were stationed on Hadrian's Wall, which stretches across modern Cumbria and Northumberland. What they were doing there, and why, emerges from the bigger story of the rise and eventual fall of the Roman Empire.

The first Roman incursions into Britain were under the command of Julius Caesar in 55 and 54 BC. They were more exploratory raids than a serious attempt to absorb these distant islands on the outer fringes of Europe into the rapidly expanding Empire. However, they served to create trading links (Britain was rich in minerals such as tin, gold, lead and iron) and client relationships with tribal leaders in the south of the country. These relationships were not always easy, and the Emperor Augustus drew up three further plans for invasion in 34, 27 and 25 BC, but was distracted by other problems. Emperor Caligula planned an invasion in AD 40, with his troops bizarrely being instructed to attack the waters of the Channel, before being ordered to collect sea shells as 'plunder'.

The permanent occupation of Britain (the Roman province of Britannia), which followed the invasion under Emperor Claudius in AD 43, was prompted by the overthrow of Verica, leader of the Atrebates tribe and friend of Rome, whose capital was Silchester, north of Basingstoke. Claudius' known landing was at Richborough on the Kent coast, accompanied by 20,000 men in four legions (2nd Augusta, 9th Hispana, 14th Gemina and 20th Valeria Victrix, with possibly some men from the 8th Augusta) together with a similar number of auxiliaries, all under the command of the Roman senator, Aulus Plautius. The force swept north across the Medway near Rochester and then the Thames to take Colchester, home of the Catuvellauni tribe and their leader, Caratacus, the man who had ousted Verica. He fled to South Wales and continued to lead the local Silures tribe against the invaders until he was betrayed and captured, and sent to Rome to be paraded triumphantly by his captors eight years later. When finally defeated, the tribe was settled in the Roman town of Caerwent in Wales whose Roman walls are still significantly intact. The Romans never fully trusted the Welsh, which is why one of Britain's most substantial legionary fortresses was built at Caerleon round AD 75, and only abandoned some 225 years later. A substantial amphitheatre and legionary barracks have been excavated, while much of the adjacent Roman town lies under modern buildings.

One of the most distinguished legionary commanders during the Claudian invasion was Vespasian, (later the Roman Emperor best remembered for the defeat of the Jewish Revolt under the command of his son Titus in AD 70.) With the 2nd Augusta he took, among others, Maiden Castle and Hod Hill, two formidable Iron Age fortresses in Dorset, which are still powerfully evocative reminders of the violent conflicts that characterized Rome's colonization of the remoter parts of Britain. He advanced further west to Exeter and possibly Bodmin. At the same time the 9th Hispana was pushing up the east coast, and secured the area up to the Humber during the next four years. Wales was to remain an ongoing problem for the Roman invaders, with resistance focused on the Druids, the Celtic priestly caste whose power base was in the north-west, on the island of Anglesey. It was during the campaign against the Druids in AD 60, by the then governor of the province, Suetonius Paulinus, that one of the most serious threats to Roman rule was launched, the Boudiccan revolt. Prasutagus, the leader of the Iceni tribe in East Anglia, died in AD 60, leaving his kingdom jointly to the Roman emperor and his daughters. Rome peremptorily seized his territory, as Roman law, unlike Celtic custom, did not recognise women as heirs. His wife Boudicca (more commonly known as Boadicea) was flogged and her daughters raped. She managed to raise the tribes of south-east England in revolt, and before Paulinus could return from Wales her forces burnt the new towns of London (Londinium), Colchester (Camulodunum) and St Albans (Verulamium), slaughtering tens of thousands. A layer of ashes from this attack has been found by archaeologists working on sites in Roman London, to the south and east of the modern Barbican development. Eventually defeated by the more disciplined Roman army, Boudicca poisoned herself and her daughters.

What gave the Roman legions their edge was not only their training and equipment, but also the network of roads, heavily fortified garrisons and marching camps that radiated out across the south of Britain, then advanced with the legions further north as they pressed on into Wales and eventually to Scotland. Rather than using existing Iron Age tracks such as the Ridgeway, legionaries surveyed and built most roads themselves, and these can still be seen cutting across the countryside, such as on Wheeldale on the North Yorkshire Moors. Their presence is often discernable by the straight lines that seem to reflect the unswerving confidence of the 'Pax Romana' – Rome's mission to bring peace, prosperity and civilisation to its subject peoples, whether they wanted it or not. There is no record of the names given by the Romans to these roads, so the names now adopted for them, such as Ermine Street, Stane Street, Watling Street and Fosse Way, are all later creations from Saxon times. References to Roman occupation still abound in towns and villages along their routes today, names such as Ancaster, Brancaster, Doncaster, Chester, Chichester and Cirencester, derived from 'castrum' (plural 'castra'), the Latin word for fort. Bridges were thrown up, aqueducts built and roads were cut, often through the harshest of landscapes, and finally the northern frontier was secured. The most northerly substantial fortification was the briefly occupied Antonine Wall in Scotland. However, a far more durable defensive line was the 73-mile long Hadrian's Wall from the Solway Firth – near Scotland's current border – to Wallsend or modern Tyneside. This extensive fortification, which uses to advantage the great rocky outcrop of the Whin Sill in its central section, was started after a visit by Emperor Hadrian in AD 122, and was still being improved at the time of his death 16 years later. Today, it forms some of the most notable Roman remains anywhere in the world.

The layouts of the principle garrison forts, such as Chesters and Housesteads, with their barrack blocks and bath complexes, are very clear from the air, and remains of numerous watch towers along the substantial vestiges of the Wall evoke a real sense of the outer edge of empire. And it was from the other outer edges of this huge empire – Syria, Iraq, Spain and Germany – that troops were sent to guard the northern frontier. As Roman citizens, or as men seeking citizenship through service with the auxiliaries, soldiers went where they were sent in this most polyglot of armies. A remarkable insight into Roman military life was discovered in the 1970s, at Chesterholm (Vindolanda), just south of the Wall. These Vindolanda letters, written on wooden tablets, are of both a personal and military nature, and were miraculously preserved in a waterlogged rubbish heap. The troops stationed there were auxiliaries or cavalry, some local Britons and some from Gaul. Invitations between wives to birthday parties were found amongst requests for additional clothing, expense accounts and much else relating to the daily life of a northern garrison in the late first and early second centuries.

The boundary of empire had been planned to run further north, well into Scotland, and in AD 80 the Roman governor Agricola, defeated the Caledonian tribes at the battle of Mons Graupius. A major legionary fortress was briefly established at Inchtuthil in AD 83, and a line of forts and signal stations was built along the Gask Ridge in Perthshire. The Antonine Wall, from the Firths of Clyde to Forth, was started under Emperor Antoninus Pius in 142. It was only ontinuously occupied for around 20 years before a withdrawal to Hadrian's Wall around the time of the Emperor's death in 161, but Scotland (Caledonia) continued to provoke Roman intervention, such as during the Brigantes revolt in 155-157, when the Antonine Wall was re-occupied briefly. There are more Roman marching camps in Scotland than anywhere else in Europe, an indication of the number of incursions by Roman expeditionary forces attempting to crush the Pictish tribes. One of the most significant was in 209 when Emperor Septimius Severus led three legions, numerous auxiliaries and fleets from Britain, the Rhineland and the Danube northwards. The legionaries ruthlessly exterminated all in their path, but suffered huge losses through guerrilla activity themselves before retreating south to Hadrian's Wall. The Emperor died in York in 211, still planning further attacks.

Many of these advances northwards were mounted from the military bases in York, founded in AD 71, and Chester, the former remaining a major military base for the much of the next two thousand years. However, Roman occupation was not about continuous warfare, and for many of the estimated three million or so inhabitants of Roman Britain, life settled down as Rome's wealthier subjects began to adopt the fashions and mores of their conquerors. Creation and cultivation, not destruction, became the focus, in towns and on the great agricultural estates. Timber and sheep-rearing often proved more profitable than arable farming for owners of these estates, which in turn relied on the expanding road network to bring their produce to market. Other exports included corn, hunting dogs and bears for Roman arenas, and slaves sourced from Ireland and Scotland.

Domestic architecture saw a wide range of comforts on offer to those who could afford them. Underfloor heating, bath houses and elaborate mosaics can still be appreciated in the extensive remains of Roman towns such as Wroxeter in Shropshire, the palace of Fishbourne in Sussex, and in many of the fine villas such as Lullingstone, Bignor, Rockbourne and North Leigh. The public temple building mania was partly to ensure the switching of loyalties from Celtic to Roman gods, while most Roman garrisons had a temple to the soldiers' god, Mithras. Christianity, too, was to arrive from the second century. The British diet became more varied, with the import of spices and foods from other parts of the empire, while Britain's oysters – and pearls were appreciated as far away as Rome. Glassware made its first appearance. Veterans married local women and settled in towns like Lincoln, where the north gate of the Roman town still bestrides the modern road, Cheltenham and Gloucester.

The continuous presence of three legions in Britain gave anyone with imperial aspirations a strong power base from which to launch their ambitions, and several had tried unsuccessfully before Constantine was declared Emperor of Britain, Gaul, Germany and Spain in York in 306, after the death of his father, the Emperor Constantius, after yet another campaign to suppress the Picts. The building from the late third century of numerous Saxon Shore forts, from Brancaster and Burgh in Norfolk to Reculver and Dover in Kent, Pevensey in Sussex and Portchester in Hampshire shows that Rome's control of its northern frontiers was no longer so secure, with seaborne raiders from Germany coming to probe Britain's defences, as Rome's focus shifted eastwards, to Germania. The Roman Empire had expanded to a point where its powers of control were simply overstretched.

By 410, it appears that there was no significant Roman military presence left in Britain, and an important episode in Britain's history came to a close, not with a bang, but with the whimper of withdrawal and retreat. That August, Alaric's Visigoths sacked Rome, and the emperor's response to pleas for help against barbarian incursions was to inform the people of Britannia that they now had to fend for themselves. The 'Dark Ages' were about to begin.

Vercovicium Roman Fort (Housesteads), Northumberland, looking west

Cilurnum (Chesters) Roman Fort and bath house, Northumberland   **159**

Banna (Birdoswald) Roman Fort and Hadrian's Wall, Cumbria, looking west

Roman watchtower on the site of Scarborough Castle, Yorkshire

Portus Adurni Roman Fort, Portchester Castle, Hampshire

Anderitum Roman Fort, Pevensey Castle, East Sussex

Viroconium Cornoviorum Roman Town, Wroxeter, Shropshire

Rutupiae Roman Fort, Richborough, Kent: likely landing place for the Roman invasion in AD 43

Roman theatre at Verulamium, St Albans, Hertfordshire

Roman amphitheatre at Caerleon, Newport, South Wales

Roman barracks, Caerleon: the fort was HQ for Legio II Augusta from 75 to 300 AD

Ham Hill, Somerset: hill fort, captured in AD 45 by the Augusta Roman legion

Garrianonum Roman cavalry fort, Burgh Castle, Norfolk

Bartlow Hills, Cambridgeshire: Romano-British burial mounds

Caerwent Roman Town, Monmouthshire, South Wales

Virosidum Roman Fort, Bainbridge, North Yorkshire

174   Charterhouse, Somerset: lead and silver mines, and Roman fort, on the Mendip Hills

Roman settlement at Charterhouse, Mendip Hills, Somerset

Roman courtyard villa, Rockbourne, Hampshire

Fishbourne Roman Palace, West Sussex: site of vast Roman building, 150 metres square

Bennachie, Aberdeenshire, Scotland: possible site of Mons Graupius Battle in AD 83

Antonine Wall, near Falkirk, Scotland: built in AD 140, between the Firths of Clyde and Forth **179**

N 54°22'07.6" W 0°45'38.2" Grid Ref: SE806977 Map Ref: 9 G3

Roman Road, Wheeldale, North Yorkshire Moors

Gask Ridge frontier, Perth & Kinross, Scotland

Stane Street, Roman road near Billingshurst, West Sussex

Ambleside, Cumbria: site of a Roman fort guarding the road from Brougham to Ravenglass

Site of Regulbium Roman Fort, Reculver, Kent, and ruins of a 14th century church

Site of Roman town of Calleva Atrebatum, Silchester, Hampshire

The Silchester Insula IX Roman Town Life Project, Calleva Atrebatum, Silchester, Hampshire **185**

The Roman town of Eboracum (York), Yorkshire

The Roman town of Camulodunum (Colchester), Essex, was the first Roman capital of Britannia **187**

The Roman town of Noviomagus Reginorum (Chichester), West Sussex

The Roman town of Durovernum Cantiacorum (Canterbury), Kent

The Roman town of Durovigutum (Godmanchester), Cambridgeshire

Traprain Law Hill Fort, Lothian, Scotland: occupied by the Votadini tribe during the Roman period **191**

192   Wansdyke at Tan Hill, Wiltshire: early medieval linear defensive earthwork built 5th-6th Centuri

FROM SAXONS TO VIKINGS
410 – 1066

rtchester Castle, the most complete remaining Roman Saxon Shore fort, had first been established some 150 ars before the Romans finally left Britain around 410. Threats from across the North Sea had been a real danger r years, and the commander of the chain of forts that protected Britain's east and south coasts had been killed in 7 as the country reeled from onslaughts by Saxons, Franks and others. Only military intervention by the Spaniard, ount Theodosius, saved the day, but respite was temporary.

e invaders from the east were made up of different tribal groupings. Angles, from the modern Danish-German rder area, invaded and settled in East Anglia, Mercia (central England) and Northumbria, slowly allying themselves th the Saxons before history paired them inseparably as the Anglo-Saxons. Jutes from Jutland and the west coast Denmark colonized Kent and the Isle of Wight. Hengist and Horsa, two Jutes hired in 449 as mercenary warlords the Romano-British authorities to help protect the country from the Picts, sent news back from their base on e Isle of Thanet that Britannia was ripe for picking. Friesians too arrived from the islands off the Dutch coast and rth-west Germany, already closely linked to the Saxons, and with a language similar to Old English. Their early volvement against the Picts ('painted ones') is recalled in the name of Dumfries (Fort of the Frisians). There were o forebears of the later Danish and Norwegian Vikings, all in all a formidable cauldron of potential and actual reats to vulnerable Britannia. The pagan Saxons from German-Dutch border area were, however, the defining rce. Some were already present as farmers during Roman times, but they arrived in overwhelming numbers in the th century, settling in what later became Essex (East Saxons), Sussex (South Saxons) and Wessex (West Saxons).

the face of such overwhelming odds, the Britons were pushed back into western England, Wales and the Strathclyde ea of Scotland. However, not everything went the invaders' way, and an Anglo-Saxon army was defeated at the ttle of Mons Badonicus, possibly somewhere near Bath, around 500. The legend of Arthur, who was possibly a tish warlord, emerged later to explain British success at this time. Several sites are still closely associated with his th, including Tintagel Castle and the Glastonbury area (Avalon). Only in 577, after the Battle of Deorham, did invaders prevail. Evidence of the culture and artistic skills of the newcomers was everywhere, including one of best-known examples of the new Anglo-Saxon art – the Sutton Hoo treasure from a ship burial site in Suffolk m around 625, with its iconic and much reconstructed helmet. Mercia and Wessex emerged as the two dominant wers, eventually uniting as a powerful Christian kingdom after Alfred the Great of Wessex's daughter, Ethelfleda, d married the king of Western Mercia around 886.

nilar confrontations were played out in Scotland, its peoples part pagan and part Christian, where the Dal Riáta ossibly 'Scotti' immigrants from Ireland) in Argyll, the Britons in Strathclyde ('Valley of the Clyde'), and the Picts the north-east across to Inverness, fought each other and the Anglians. The Anglian Kingdom of Northumbria, ich was only established by the Anglo-Saxons after 550, included land up to the Forth. In the mid-eighth century, e Picts seized the strategic fortress of Dunadd in Argyll, but the Dal Riáta Scotti retook it and reversed the tables by ntury's end, giving their name to a country unified under Kenneth MacAlpine in the ninth century – Scotland.

The Venerable Bede, who lived about 673 to 735, was the most noted historian of the age, and an articulate propagan[dist] for the new Saxon order from his monastery in Jarrow on the Tyne. His *Ecclesiastical History of the English Peo[ple]*, which covers the time from Julius Caesar to the completion of the book in 731, is an essential sourcebook for histor[ians] of the period. He vigorously lauded the efforts of St Augustine of Canterbury to reintroduce Roman Christianit[y to] Britain from 596, yet ignored the efforts of St Patrick and others who had kept Christianity alive in the previous [two] hundred years in Ireland and the north and west of England, despite the waves of pagan invaders. He was eventu[ally] buried in Durham Cathedral and later canonised.

King Offa of Mercia further secured his western border with Wales with the massive Offa's Dyke earthwork, lo[ng] and to the east of the seventh and eighth century Wansdyke. He organised defences in Kent in 792 against a new w[ave] of seaborne invaders, the Vikings, Norse raiders from modern Norway and Denmark. The first significant indica[tion] of the problems ahead was in 793 in Northumbria, where the monastery of Lindisfarne was attacked by Norwe[gian] Vikings. The desecration of St Cuthbert's shrine, and the massacre of many of the monks by pagan barbarians, se[nt a] shudder through Christendom. Initially raids were sporadic and probably opportunistic, but the Vikings' confide[nce] grew as they probed down the east coast, attacking Jarrow – unsuccessfully this time – in 794, as well as raiding [islands] off the west coast. The Isle of Sheppey in the Thames estuary was overwhelmed in 835. In the early ninth cen[tury] they also seized the Shetlands, Orkney and the Faroes, ousting the Irish monks who had preceded them by at lea[st a] century, before focusing increasingly on the west coast. The Brough of Birsay, a tidal island on Orkney's north-w[est] coast, has extensive Viking remains.

The Isle of Man became an important Viking centre, as did the Isle of Anglesey, though Dublin was to become t[he] main base and trading port for all kinds of merchandise, especially slaves, sourced from their own raids as far a[way] as North Africa and Italy. The Danes first launched their raiding armies in the mid-ninth century: a new player [had] entered the fray. Unlike earlier raiders, they did not limit their activities to the coasts and river systems, but ra[nged] widely across the country. They picked their moment well, as the English were involved in internecine warfare, [and] before long Northumbria fell to them in 867, followed by East Anglia in 870 and Mercia in 877. Estimates of the [size] of this 'Great Army' vary widely, from 10,000 to 40,000 men. Despite the Danes being defeated in 871 at Ashd[own] they retreated to Basing where they defeated King Aethelred, who died soon after. The new king, Alfred the G[reat] (871-899) was forced to pay tribute – 'Danegeld' – as Wessex was too weak to resist. The Danes turned their atten[tion] to Mercia for the next few years, by which time Guthrum had succeeded in conquering all but Wessex. In 876 [the] Danes seized Wareham, Exeter in 877 and Chippenham in January 878. Although Alfred had avoided capture, he [was] still forced to seek refuge in the Somerset Fens. Regrouping near Athelney, he struck back and defeated the Dan[es at] Countisbury Hill (Devon) and Edington (Wiltshire) before forcing them to surrender at Chippenham in May 878[.]

A peace treaty, the Treaty of Wedmore, was concluded with Guthrum, who was baptized a Christian as Athels[tan.] Guthrum broke the treaty in 884 but was defeated again. London, where the Anglo-Saxons had settled west of the w[alls] of the largely abandoned Roman city – around the Strand and Covent Garden in 'Lundenwic' – was also libera[ted.] In 886 it was agreed (in the 'Treaty of Alfred and Guthrum') that the country would be split between Wessex [and] Danelaw, the eastern part of the country between the Thames and the Tees rivers, north of Watling Street com[ing] under Danish control. Four out of five Danelaw boroughs would later become county towns: Derby, Leicester, Lin[coln] and Nottingham. Urban centres expanded significantly under Viking rule, from less than a dozen to around a hun[dred] by the time of the Norman invasion.

lfred consolidated his defences on land and sea, as raids continued into the 890s. He set up a network of burghs – rtified towns – an initiative that renewed urban settlement after years of atrophy in the wake of Roman withdrawal. ome towns, such as London, York, Ipswich and Hamwic (near Southampton), had remained important trading ntres for whoever controlled them, but the new initiative reorganized former Roman centres such as Winchester, hichester, Exeter, Bath, and Portchester. Structured street layouts were reintroduced, as well as the metalling of ads, using flint, which in Winchester covered over five miles of roads. However, populations were small: London der 20,000, Lincoln perhaps 5,000, and medium-sized towns like Colchester about 2,500. Along the Thames ere were fortified frontier towns at Cricklade, Oxford and Wallingford. Mercia and Wales were cultivated as lies through marriage and strategic relationships. Drawing on existing Kentish and Mercian laws, Alfred set about tablishing a definitive set of Anglo-Saxon legal codes, and tried to curtail the practice of blood feuds. Sharing with ede and Gildas the belief that the Vikings were a divine punishment visited on the English for their sins, Alfred omoted religious study and learnt Latin.

anelaw was finally absorbed by Alfred's son, Edward the Elder, into Wessex by 918. The Scotti, Strathclyde and orthumbria all submitted to Edward in 920, though in 937 the Scotti and Dublin Norse allied against Alfred's andson, Athelstan of Wessex, but were defeated with the aid of Mercia at Brunanburh (possibly Bromborough on e Wirral). It was he who styled himself 'King of the English' on his coinage. York enjoyed increased prosperity from e peace treaty, thus becoming the target of further Viking raids. It remained an Irish-Norse town, sometimes allied and sometimes in conflict with Wessex, until Eric 'Bloodaxe' was expelled in 954. Generally though the tenth ntury was relatively quiet: Anglo-Saxon peasantry scraped a living from the land from subsistence farming, and life ay not have been radically different from the late Iron Age. Some would have moved into the former Roman estates, d there is evidence that some villas were maintained for long periods after the Romans departed. In some of the ore remote regions, such as the Scottish Highlands and the Welsh mountains, life went on relatively undisturbed the depredations of the Viking armies, as indeed had also been the case in Roman times. Livestock and arable rming were the mainstays, and most clothes would have been home-made, from wool or flax. The characteristic rip field patterns at sites like Midlem near Selkirk and Ditchford in Gloucestershire, can still be seen clearly from e air. Surviving artefacts reveal the Vikings as a visually sophisticated society, though there are strange gaps, such an almost total lack of Scandinavian ceramics. Chester, a prosperous Irish-Norse trading post, developed the eciality of minting coinage, although it was sacked in 890 when the Viking raids resumed. Where finds are made, ch as the Croydon hoard and Cuerdale treasure chest, the contents emphasize the international scope of Viking ading and raiding, with coins from the Carolingian Empire and the Arab world, as well as throughout Britain.

helred came to the throne of Wessex in 991, and was faced immediately with a large Norwegian invasion et. Ethelred's defeat at the Battle of Maldon led to England being saddled with paying Danegeld to get rid of e Norwegian fleet. Ethelred's son, Edmund Ironside, succeeded in 1016, sharing the throne with Canute (Knut), ready King of Norway and Denmark. By 1017 Canute had seized East Anglia from the Saxons, but defeat in the ttle of Carham gave territory north of the River Tweed to Scotland. Canute took over a country that was relatively osperous, with a stable currency and expanding population, and an established administrative coherence through e shire system. Canute's two sons, Harold Harefoot and Harthacanute, succeeded to the throne in turn. Their igns were short and violent, and the way was then open for Edward the Confessor (1042-1066), son of Ethelred, d the scene was set for 1066 and an invasion that was to transform England.

196   Glastonbury Abbey, Somerset: a community of monks was founded here as early as AD 63

stonbury Tor, Somerset: occupied since Neolithic, with mystical significance since 1st century AD **197**

Iona, Inner Hebrides, Scotland: cradle for christianity in Scotland and northern England

Iona Abbey, Inner Hebrides, Scotland: in 563, St Columba founded a monastery here

200 Lindisfarne Priory, Holy Island, Northumberland: founded around 635 by St Aidan, from Iona

...arne Islands, Northumberland: early dwelling place for monks from Lindisfarne seeking hermitage **201**

202 Framlingham Castle, Suffolk: a castle was here in 600, but the current ruin dates from 12th centur

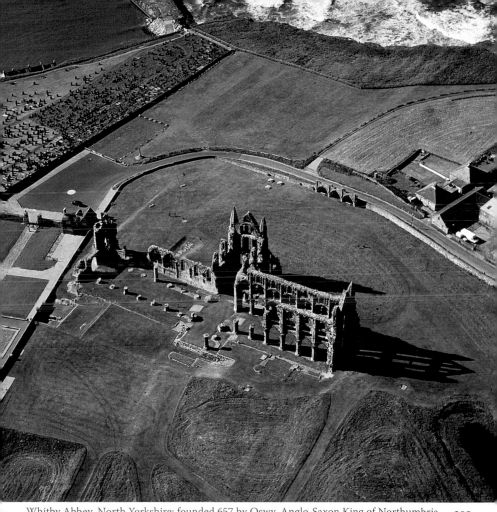

Whitby Abbey, North Yorkshire: founded 657 by Oswy, Anglo-Saxon King of Northumbria **203**

204 Westminster Abbey: the first stone abbey was built here around 1050 by King Edward the Confessor

Tintagel, Cornwall: traces of an early monastery dating back to 5th or 6th centuries

206   Muchelney Abbey, Somerset : religious site since 693, then Benedictine monks came in 10th cent

Offa's Dyke, near Mainstone, Shropshire

208 Bury St Edmunds Abbey, Suffolk: a shrine to St Edmund, Saxon King murdered by Danes in 869

Tynemouth Priory, Tyne and Wear: founded in 7th century but destroyed by Danes in 875

210   Ashmore, Dorset: an upland village occupied since Roman times, built around an embanked pon•

Anglesey, Wales: invaded by pirates from Ireland, British warlords, Vikings and Saxons **211**

212   Jarlshof, Shetland: ruins include a Bronze Age smithy, Iron Age broch, and Viking longhouses

Brough of Deerness, Orkney: a pre-Norse chapel and other human traces of unknown age   **213**

214   Brough of Birsay, Orkney: settled in 5th century, later a Pictish fort, then taken by Norsemen

Scone Castle, Scotland: an ancient gathering site for Picts, later a place of coronation of kings 215

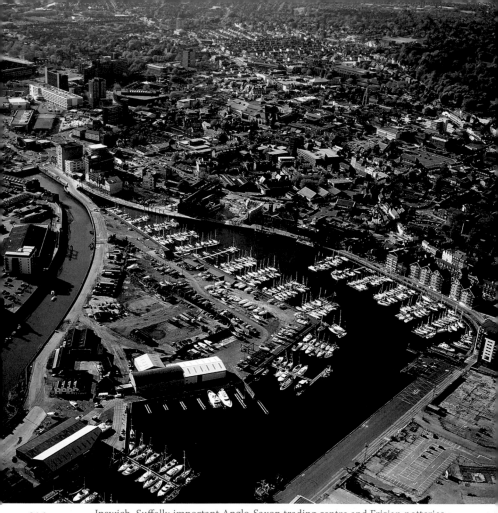

Ipswich, Suffolk: important Anglo-Saxon trading centre and Frisian potteries

xford University: established by end of 11th century but a place of scholarship from Saxon times 217

218 Godwick, Norfolk: deserted site of village established in Saxon times

Saxon Fields near Draycott, Somerset

Castle Acre Castle, Norfolk: a motte and bailey castle, founded in 11th century

THE NORMAN CONQUEST
1066 - 1154

he military expedition that crossed the English Channel from northern France by night, landing at Pevensey on
e morning of 28 September 1066, was to lead to a battle that has become probably the best-known date in English
story. The battle of Hastings is rightly remembered as one of the most significant ever to have been fought on
nglish soil, but it was merely a prelude to the massive political, military, social and cultural changes that were to
ve profound consequences for the future history of the whole of Britain. Led by Duke William of Normandy,
e expedition could be described as the completion of the Viking conquest of England, as the powerful state of
ormandy had been founded by Norsemen some 150 years earlier.

illiam was a fighter, an illegitimate son, who had succeeded to the dukedom at the age of seven. He had fought to
ercome internal unrest as well as external threats and his army was a formidable force of horsemen and archers,
illed in the arts of war. The expedition was the result of his ambition to take the throne of England, an ambition
cused and sharpened by the death of the English king, Edward the Confessor, on 5 January 1066. Edward had died
ildless, apparently less interested in dynastic considerations than in the rebuilding of a Benedictine monastery on
e island of Thorney in the River Thames outside the western gate of the city of London. The monastery – known
the 'West Minster' – was completed just before his death and was to be his burial-place. The English court had
rong links to Normandy, but inevitably Edward's death created a dangerous vacuum, and this was to give William
e excuse he needed to take what he believed was his lawful inheritance, the inheritance that had been promised
m by Edward in 1051. But unknown events at the court of the dying king at Christmas 1065 changed Edward's
nd, and Harold of Wessex, the son of Earl Godwin, was proclaimed Edward's heir. A third man, Harold Hardrada
Norway, was also casting covetous eyes towards England, and so the stage was set for a power struggle.

nd the kingdom of England was a prize worth having, rich and powerful. The institutions of law and justice
re long established, together with a system of local government and taxation. The currency was silver pennies
oduced by skilled metal workers whose artistry was renowned across Western Europe. The land was fertile and
ll watered, with plentiful supplies of timber, and with monasteries and parish churches to serve the spiritual needs
the people.

e day after Edward died, Harold, son of Godwin, was crowned king. In the few troubled months of his reign he
vealed himself to be a highly competent leader and a formidable opponent in battle. His test came soon when
May 1066 he saw off a raid by his half-brother, Tostig, on the south coast. Thinking this to be a preliminary to a
l-blown invasion by William, Harold gathered all the available ships and men to meet an attack. But the attack
ver came and in early September he was disbanding his forces when the news came that Tostig had allied himself
th Harold Hardrada and had landed on the Yorkshire coast. He immediately reassembled his men and speedily
rched north to meet the Norwegian army. The battle came at Stamford Bridge near York with the English king
nning a great and decisive victory that ended both the threat of attack from the north as well as revolt from within
rold's own family. Both Tostig and Harold Hardrada were killed and the tattered remnants of their army returned
Norway. But Harold had little time to savour his triumph before messengers brought news of William's landing on

the south coast. William had established a base at Hastings, and there he and his forces lay in wait. On the night of Friday, 13 October, Harold encamped his army in a good defensive position some nine miles from Hastings at the top of a slope that was backed by the great forest of the Weald, a site now occupied by the ruins of Battle Abbey. The Norman army left Hastings and began the attack early on the Saturday morning. The fighting lasted until dusk fell, and it was a battle that Harold very nearly won, the shield wall and axes of the English army initially holding firm against the might of the Norman cavalry. The critical point came when the Normans appeared to be in retreat, causing some of the English to break ranks. The Norman cavalry reformed, seizing the advantage, and despite fierce fighting throughout the day the Normans gained ground as the number of English dead steadily increased. As dusk was coming on, Harold himself was killed – tradition has it by an arrow piercing his eye – and his army was scattered.

But although he had won a military victory, William was still far from the crown of England. His first move was to retreat to his stronghold at Hastings and gather reinforcements, as well as strengthening and garrisoning the fortifications at Dover in case he needed to make a rapid withdrawal, and then to march on London – a thriving commercial centre – by a circuitous route, laying the countryside to waste as he went. Unable to take London, he continued westwards and then southwards to Winchester, where the royal treasury was. His move northwards on the Icknield Way demonstrated his increasing confidence that there was to be no effective military opposition from the English. At Little Berkhampstead, a few of the surviving Saxon earls, together with the Archbishop of York and representatives from London, met William and offered him their submission and the throne of England. On Christmas Day, less than a year after the death of Edward the Confessor, William was crowned king in Westminster Abbey. But although king, William was still not recognized across the country and resistance continued. He responded in a typically ruthless fashion, devastating large areas of the Midlands and the North with the result that the Vale of York was effectively rendered a wasteland and remained so for decades afterwards.

The old Saxon nobility was replaced by William's men across the country. Norman power had to be demonstrated by military presence, a visible and recognizable reminder of the conquest and the new order. The invaders also needed to establish secure administrative centres in areas of high population. The Normans were great castle builders and a programme of castle building was begun, typically motte and bailey constructions, where a motte or earth mound was thrown up and topped by a stockade or keep. An encircling or adjacent enclosure – the bailey – was created by digging out a ditch and forming a rampart. Initially, many of these early Norman castles were wooden constructions. The materials for wooden castles were often readily available, they could be built easily and easily dismantled in case of retreat. But the preference of the Normans was always for stone and gradually as their grip tightened on the country, the wooden fortifications were replaced by permanent stone structures, their external walls often plastered and painted white in order to emphasize their size and solidity. By the end of the eleventh century, hundreds of castles had been built in England. Many of these symbols of the Norman achievement can still be seen in the landscape, and many became the focus for later settlement and development.

In London alone, William built three castles, the most famous of which is the Tower of London on the banks of the Thames. Carisbrooke Castle on the Isle of Wight was begun scarcely four years after the Battle of Hastings, and its motte and bailey are still plainly visible. The massive keep of Colchester demonstrates an interesting historical continuity: the castle was built on the site of the old Roman temple of Claudius, and some of the original brick from the temple were reused in its construction. The work of Roman builders also proved useful at Lincoln. William ordered the construction of a castle there in 1068 and the remains of the old Roman walls formed the enclosure of the outer bailey.

The marches of Scotland and Wales – the border areas – were to remain unsettled regions for many years, and the possession of key sites there were critical to the maintenance of Norman power. Where they could, they chose a site that combined natural advantages with a strategic location. Bamburgh Castle in Northumbria, which was captured and refortified by William's son, William Rufus, takes advantage of the local geology, being built on the top of a basalt outcrop by the coast, while Pembroke Castle in south Wales is built in a superb defensive site on a rocky promontory, evidence of the Normans' determination to put their mark on as much of Britain as they could.

These castles developed many functions as the first wooden structures were rebuilt in stone. Originally designed as garrisons, the base from which a cavalry force could conduct its operations in the surrounding countryside and to which it could retreat if necessary, castles evolved into highly sophisticated military centres, combining a multiplicity of roles: a residence for the local magnate and his retainers, a barracks, a courthouse, a gaol for prisoners, a storehouse, a strong-room, stables and an administrative centre. The establishment of a castle attracted settlement outside its walls, craftsmen and traders, and these settlements were in some cases later to became significant towns even after the importance of the castle to which they owned their origins had long vanished.

One of the areas upon which the Norman Conquest had an almost immediate impact was the church. By the time William died in 1087, all the bishops except for one were Norman appointees. The exception was the saintly Wulfstan of Worcester, who had early come to an accommodation with William, managing to combine loyalty to the king with loyalty to the church. Many of the abbots, the heads of the monasteries, were also replaced. If the Normans were keen to build castles, symbols of their temporal power, they were also keen to demonstrate their spiritual authority. Their formidable energies were put to work rebuilding the old Saxon churches and constructing cathedrals. In sharp contrast to the more modest Saxon designs, these new cathedrals were massive buildings within which the newcomers could indulge their love of procession and ceremonial. One of these is Durham, sited on a hill in a deep bend of the River Wear that gives it the appearance of being on an island dominating the surrounding landscape. The great abbey church at Ely that rises above the fenland of East Anglia was begun in the late eleventh century. It was to become the cathedral, the seat of the bishop, with the creation of a diocese that was carved out of the huge diocese of Lincoln in 1109. The Saxon cathedral at Canterbury was burnt down in 1067. The first Norman archbishop of Canterbury, Lanfranc, started the rebuilding, which was completed by the next archbishop, Anselm. It was to be the final scene of a conflict between William's great grandson, Henry II, and his archbishop, Thomas Becket, when Thomas was assassinated by four of Henry's knights in 1170. Although a second fire at Canterbury destroyed the church, the crypt beneath the cathedral survived – a fine example of the Norman mason's art. William also commissioned a land valuation and survey in 1087 – the Domesday Book – which hold records of 13,418 settlements in England – a unique picture of eleventh century England.

An altogether different memorial to Norman energy is in Hampshire where a great tract of land – the New Forest – was set aside so that the king and his barons could pursue their love of hunting. It is still possible to wander in the quiet glades of this forest, which has remained largely unchanged for a thousand years.

224 Dover Castle, Kent: the present castle dates back to 12th century, on a site occupied from the Iron

Battle Abbey, East Sussex: built on the site of the 1066 Battle of Hastings

226 Carisbrooke Castle, Isle of Wight: dates from 11th century, on a site occupied since Roman times

228 Chepstow Castle, Monmouthshire: built in 1067 and one of the oldest stone fortifications in Brita

Norwich Castle, Norfolk: found in 1067 as a timber fort, built in stone in 12th century

Warwick Castle: originally a mott and bailey, the present castle dates back to 13th century

232   Stafford Castle: built as a motte and bailey with timber fortification, later rebuilt in stone

Richmond Castle, Yorkshire: founded in 1071 following the brutal 'harrowing of the north' in 1069 **233**

Windsor Castle, Berkshire: dates from 11th century, the largest inhabited castle in the world

Tower of London: a fortress, royal palace and prison, dates back to 1078

236 St Albans Cathedral, Hertfordshire: dates from 11th century, on the site commemorating Alban

Rochester Cathedral, Kent: dates from 12th century

238   Ely Cathedral, Cambridgeshire: dates from 11th century on the site of a Saxon monastery

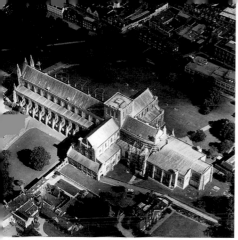

Winchester Cathedral, Hampshire

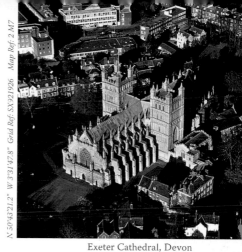

Exeter Cathedral, Devon

N 50°43'21.2" W 3°31'47.8" Grid Ref: SX921926 Map Ref: 2 M7

Lincoln Cathedral, Lincolnshire

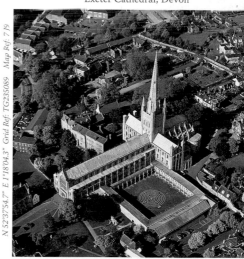

Norwich Cathedral, Norfolk

N 52°37'54.7" E 1°18'04.3" Grid Ref: TG235089 Map Ref: 7 J9

240 Lewes Castle: a mott and bailey castle, built in 1087 with timber fortification, later rebuilt in stor

Cardiff Castle, Glamorgan, Wales: dates back to 1091, built on the site of a Roman fortification **241**

Corfe Castle, Dorset: built on a former Saxon site in 11th century

Pembroke Castle, Pembrokeshire, Wales: built in 1093, during the Norman Conquest of Wales **243**

244 Durham Cathedral (11th to 12th centuries) and Durham Castle (early motte and bailey castle)

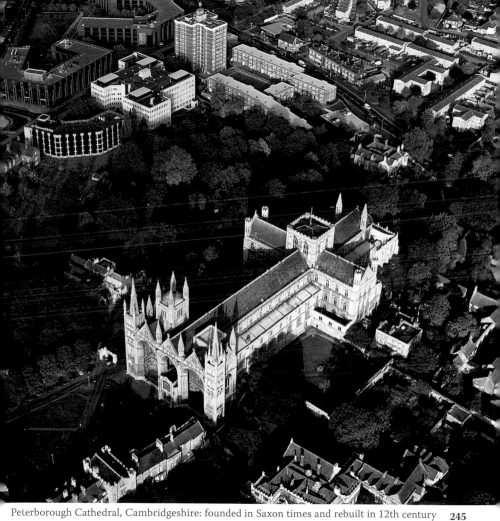

Peterborough Cathedral, Cambridgeshire: founded in Saxon times and rebuilt in 12th century 245

Castle Acre Priory, Norfolk: founded in 1089

Yielden Castle, Bedfordshire: a mott and bailey castle with two baileys, built in 12th century **247**

248 Llansteffan Castle, Camarthenshire, Wales: built in 12th century on the site of a Neolithic fort

Carew Castle, Pembrokeshire, Wales: built in early 12th century on the site of an Iron Age fort **249**

Leeds Castle, Kent: built in 1119, on the site of a Saxon manor house

Arundel Castle, West Sussex: built in 1068 as a motte and bailey, later lavishly extended

252 Rievaulx Abbey, Yorkshire: the first Cistercian abbey in the north of England, founded in 1132

Fountains Abbey, Yorkshire: the largest Cistercian monastic ruin in England, founded in 1132   **253**

254 Tintern Abbey, Monmouthshire, Wales: the first Cistercian abbey in Wales, founded in 1131

Botolph's Priory (first Augustinian), Colchester, Essex

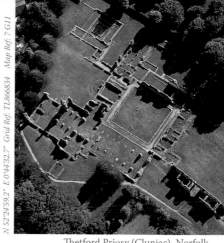

N 52°24'59.2" E 0°44'32.7"   Grid Ref: TL866834   Map Ref: 7 G11

Thetford Priory (Cluniac), Norfolk

Easby Abbey (Premonstratensian), North Yorkshire

N 54°12'10.6" W 1°09'31.9"   Grid Ref: SE550789   Map Ref: 9 E4

Byland Abbey (Cistercian), North Yorkshire

256 Scarborough Castle, North Yorkshire: built in 12th century on a site previously fortified

Ludlow Castle, Shropshire: built in 11th century as a border stronghold on the Welsh Marches **257**

Melrose Abbey, Borders, Scotland: founded in 1136 by Cistercian monks

Brinkburn Priory (Augustinian), Northumberland

N 50°50'33.4" W 2°54'41.4" Grid Ref: ST359052 Map Ref: 3 B7

Forde Abbey (Cistercian), Dorset

Buckfast Abbey (Cistercian), Devon

N 55°34'35.8" W 2°38'58.2" Grid Ref: NT591316 Map Ref: 11 E5

Dryburgh Abbey (Premonstratensian), Scotland

Castle Rising Castle, Norfolk: a magnificent Norman keep, built in 1138

Restenneth Priory, Borders, Scotland: an Augustinian monastic house, founded in 1153 **261**

262 Beaumaris Castle, Anglesey, Wales: built by Edward I in 1295 during his campaign against the W

MANORS AND MONASTERIES
1154 - 1485

he early fourteenth century, a wealthy Lincolnshire man, Sir Geoffrey Luttrell, commissioned an illustrated book, Luttrell Psalter; for the historian, its value lies in its images that open a window on to a long-vanished agricultural ld. If the king and his barons governed the country, they were dependent ultimately on the ordinary men and nen who kept it fed. Here is demonstrated the backbreaking work involving men and women, young and old, that the primary occupation of most inhabitants of Britain in the centuries following the Norman Conquest.

ough the Norman Conquest did not result in a mass influx of settlers from Normandy, it nevertheless impacted me across all levels of society and included the introduction of a type of feudalism. This was the social system that : people hard at work. Essentially it was a series of rights and obligations, with the king at its head, relating to the session of land, which extended through the barons and knights, down to the peasants – the country people. The ins and knights administered their lands through manors, sometimes made up of one or two villages. A prosperous sant was one with about 30 acres of land to cultivate, while the semi-free serf worked for the landowner, the local , in exchange for the right to cultivate an area of land to support himself and his family.

h of Britain was still forested at this time. The Anglo-Norman kings' obsession with hunting meant that huge s – possibly as much as a third of England – were designated as reserves for their exclusive use. Known as Royal sts, these reached their greatest extent under Henry II (1154-1189) and included broadleaf forests as well as heath moorland, where game animals and birds could flourish. Anyone caught in a Royal Forest poaching protected ials, enclosing land to pasture animals or clearing land for agricultural use – assarting – was subject to the harsh ishment specified under forest law, which could include mutilation and death. Bowland Forest in Lancashire is xample of a former royal forest, as is Sherwood Forest in Nottinghamshire and Epping Forest in Essex, to name a few. However, large acres of forest were expensive to manage and in order to maintain the supply of game more iomically, deer parks, large enclosed areas within the forests, were developed, Radholme Park being the first such osure in Bowland.

ting was responsible for the death in the New Forest in 1100 of the son of William I, William Rufus – William Red – so called because of his ruddy face. He was succeeded by Henry I. Astute, able and ruthless, Henry ruled and and Normandy for 35 years and it was during his reign that the beginnings of a centralized government inistration were established. A succession dispute between his daughter, Matilda, and Henry's nephew, Stephen, ght about civil war in England – the Anarchy – lasting until 1154 when Henry II was crowned king of England.

first in the line of what later came to be known as the Plantagenet kings – a line that was to endure until 1485 enry was a dynamic and outstanding figure, restoring law and order to the country. He reinstated and developed system of itinerant justices introduced by his grandfather from which the later assize courts developed. He was an efficient soldier and strategist, destroying those castles – such as Farnham and Reading – that had been ally built during the Anarchy, confiscating others and building yet more. Dover is testimony to his energy – a sprawling fortification on the hill above the Channel, an innovation in castle design, with two curtain walls unding a massive central keep. Castles such as these were designed to impress both his enemies outside his

kingdom as well as the barons within it, and remind them that power lay with the king and not with them. Or[f]
Castle, for example, on the coast of Suffolk provided a counterbalance to the local might of the Bigod family wh[ose]
stronghold was at Framlingham.

The Luttrell Psalter shows a range of different methods by which a living could be made from the land. The whole c[ycle]
of ploughing, sowing, tending the young crop and harvesting is accurately observed: the ploughman has to use b[oth]
hands to hold down the heavy plough to achieve the right depth of furrow, while his assistant urges on the plough te[am]
of four oxen with a whip. If agriculture was hard enough for those living in the arable-growing areas of lowland Brit[ain]
it was even harder for those whose homes were in the highland areas of Scotland and Wales, and this is reflecte[d in]
the population estimates. By 1300, the population of England was probably around five million, an increase of poss[ibly]
more than three million from the late eleventh century, the expansion in arable farming making it possible to sup[port]
more people. By contrast, in Wales the population was probably considerably less than 500,000; in Scotland it [was]
between 500,000 and a million. The appropriation of arable land by the Norman settlers in the Welsh valleys wh[ich]
they had gained control had forced the native Welsh into a much harder existence in the mountains.

Britain may be divided into two broad areas – the Highland and Lowland zones, respectively north-west and so[uth-]
east of a line between the River Tees as it enters the North Sea and the River Exe in Devon. Generally speaking,[the]
much older rocks of the north and west of the country, and the higher rainfall, have led to a different agricult[ural]
development from the drier and lowland areas of south and east of the country, with arable farming being m[ainly]
concentrated in the latter area. These geological and topographical differences have influenced the type of settlem[ent]
– isolated farmsteads were more usual in the north and west with large areas of upland and moorland where past[oral]
farming was carried out, while in the south and east villages tended to develop since a degree of cooperation betw[een]
groups of people was necessary to clear and maintain large areas of land under cultivation.

The greater political stability of the Anglo-Norman period also stimulated a revival in monasticism. Across the cou[ntry]
a network of religious houses was spread from Aberconwy in North Wales to Deer in Scotland, down throug[h the]
borders and right across the length and breadth of England. Some, such as Tewkesbury, were in town centres, w[hile]
others, Rievaulx for example, were in remote locations. One monastic order, the Cistercians, developed an effic[ient]
method of land management through a system of outlying granges or farms. In particular, they bred sheep whose w[ool]
– both as raw material and finished cloth – helped to lay the foundations of medieval wealth. The wool trade w[ould]
stimulate the development of towns such as Lavenham in Suffolk and Burford in Oxfordshire.

Challenges to the power of the monarchy began in 1215 when King John, Henry II's son, was compelled by the ba[rons]
to sign an agreement at Runnymede – the Magna Carta – that spelled out a series of rights that the monarch under[took]
to observe. They continued during the reign of John's son, Henry III (1216-1272). His successor, Edward I (1272-13[07])
busied himself with a massive programme of castle building in Wales including Conwy, Beaumaris, Caernarvon [and]
Harlech, and mounted military campaigns in Scotland. In 1284, Edward annexed Wales, but resistance to En[glish]
rule continued. Attempting to assert authority west and north of the border was expensive and consequentl[y his]
son, Edward II, was saddled with heavy debt. He also failed to come up to the expectation of the barons as a mil[itary]
leader and in 1314, seven years after his accession, he was roundly beaten by the Scots at Bannockburn. His succe[ssor]
Edward III, not only conducted military campaigns in Scotland but also became embroiled in what became kn[own]
as the Hundred Years War over remaining English possessions in France. It was a profoundly unsettled period

rnally and externally. Although a Scottish invasion was blocked, and the heir to the Scottish throne captured in 5, a serious uprising in Wales resulted in most of it falling under Owain Glendwr's control with the loss of many he royal castles in the borders. The fifteenth century was dominated by civil war between two rival groups to throne, the houses of York and Lancaster, ending when the Yorkist king, Richard III, was defeated at the Battle osworth in August 1485 by the Lancastrian claimant, Henry Tudor. Crowned as Henry VII, he then married abeth of York, thus uniting the two rival dynasties. The Tudor rose combines their two emblems – the red rose of caster and the white rose of York.

e landscape of Britain is littered with many castles – the relics of the power struggles of the secular lords during period – it also contains witnesses to another type of power – that of the church. Most of the great cathedrals built or rebuilt during the later middle ages. The Romanesque cathedral at Canterbury conveniently burned n in 1174, allowing for the construction of a much grander shrine church to Thomas Becket, able to process dily the large numbers of pilgrims who flocked there to pray to the saint. The cathedrals of Salisbury and Wells rise re their cities, while Winchester huddles down, its unpretentious exterior belying the size of the interior. St David's ales is built on a site of strategic importance on the route to Ireland. This was also the age of the parish church, the sh being the smallest unit of ecclesiastical administration, and hundreds were built throughout the country.

cally, crops were grown in large fields – the open field system – whereby each un-hedged field was divided into strips, each some eight metres wide and two hundred metres long. One individual might cultivate a number of s scattered throughout the village. The open-field system approximates to the more prosperous Lowland zone of ain, although in parts of Kent and Essex small enclosed fields occurred, relics of a pre Roman system. Similarly, in orth and west of Britain, the Highland zone, closed fields were common. Laxton in Nottinghamshire is one of the ew remaining open field systems in use – a relic of an agricultural and land-holding system that was to undergo ficant change in the following centuries as the land began to be enclosed. One village that seems frozen in time pleton-le-Moors in Yorkshire, its layout seeming to typify a medieval settlement with fields extending behind ong garden plots.

memorial to countless thousands lies in the very landscape of the country as it is today. It was these unnamed le who dug the ditches that helped to drain the Somerset Levels, whose ploughs created the characteristic ridge furrow pattern that is still visible in numerous sites across the country, such as the strip lynchets near Uploders in et; those people whose repeated journeys between home and field built up the network of lanes and small roads crisscross the landscape.

e-scale social and demographic change affecting the whole population occurred when the Black Death or plague ed the south coast of England in June 1348. By September it had reached London, and at the beginning of 1349 s spreading into the Midlands. Eventually, all areas of Britain, including Wales and Scotland, were affected. It ndiscriminate in its visitation and the mortality was high: an estimated 45 per cent of the population died. The ts were long-lasting, as fields lay waste with no one to work them and settlements were abandoned. The lack of r meant that for the first time the peasants could command higher wages – the breakdown of the feudal system mminent. Trade declined, with a resultant economic depression, which in turn affected urban development. ever, the coming of the Tudors heralded changes that would profoundly alter society – the first stirrings of ern Britain.

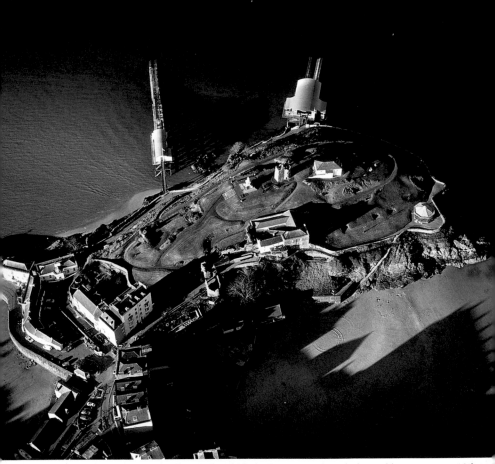

266   Tenby Castle, Pembrokeshire, Wales: dates back to 1153, though the visible remains are 13th cer

Andrews Castle, Fife, Scotland: founded in 12th century, the castle now standing is 14th century **267**

Wells Cathedral, Somerset: founded in 10th century and largely complete by 1239

Cleeve Abbey (Cistercian), Somerset

N 54°49'05.3" W 1°32'25.4" Grid Ref: NZ296471 Map Ref: 11 K11

Finchale Priory (Benedictine), Durham

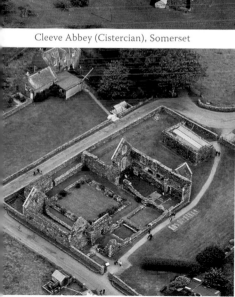

Iona Nunnery (Benedictine), Island of Iona, Scotland

N 50°49'17.3" W 1°27'00.8" Grid Ref: SU388026 Map Ref: 3 I7

Beaulieu Abbey (Cistercian), Hampshire

N 53°29′03.6″ W 1°13′33.6″ Grid Ref: SK515989 Map Ref: 9 E10

Conisbrough Castle, South Yorkshire

Middleham Castle, North Yorkshire

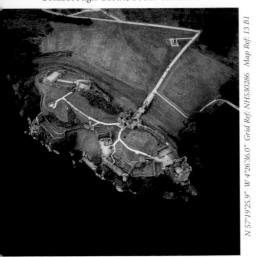

N 57°19′25.9″ W 4°26′36.0″ Grid Ref: NH530286 Map Ref: 13 B1

Urquhart Castle, Inverness-shire, Scotland

Nunney Castle, Somerset

Carreg Cennen Castle, Camarthenshire, Wales: built in 12th century on a spectacular cliff face **271**

Tioram Castle, Highlands, Scotland: dates back to 13th century

Eilean Donan Castle, Western Highlands, Scotland: built in 1220

274 Cambridge University, Cambridge, Cambridgeshire: founded in 1209 by scholars from Oxford

Salisbury Cathedral, Wiltshire: consecrated in 1258, and has the tallest church spire in Britain

276 Criccieth Castle, Caernarvonshire, Wales: built in 13th century to campaign against the English

Beeston Castle, Cheshire: built in 1224 on a site occupied since Neolithic times

278   Montgomery Castle, Montgomeryshire: built in 1073, one of many guarding the Welsh Marches.

Warkworth Castle: originally a 12th century motte and bailey castle, rebuilt in 16th century **279**

280   Duart Castle, island of Mull, Scotland: the seat of Clan MacLean, dates back to 13th century

Caerlaverock Castle, Scotland: a triangular moated castle, dates back to 13th century

282 Castell Dinas Bran, Denbighshire, Wales: built in 13th century on the site of an Iron Age fort

Caerphilly Castle, Glamorgan, South Wales: the largest castle in Wales, built in 1271

284   Aberystwyth Castle, Ceredigion: built in 1277 by Edward I during his campaign against the We

Flint Castle, Flintshire: built in 1277, the first by Edward I in his campaign against the Welsh

286   Berwick-upon-Tweed: changed hands many times between England & Scotland from 1147 to 1

Conwy Castle, Conwy, North Wales: built in 1283 for Edward I's second campaign in Wales

288 Caernarfon Castle, Gwynedd, Wales: built in 1283 during Edward I's second campaign in Wales

Harlech Castle, Gwynedd, Wales: built in 1283 during Edward I's second campaign in Wales

Loch Leven Castle, Perth & Kinross, Scotland: dates back to 13th century

Stokesay Castle, Shropshire: the oldest fortified manor house in England, built in 12th century **291**

292   Stirling Castle, dates back to 13th century, main parts seen today are from 15th & 16th centur[i]

Dunottar Castle, Aberdeenshire: a 13th century castle on the site of an earlier fortress   **293**

Otterburn, Northumberland: site of the Battle of Otterburn in 1388

Lavenham, Suffolk: a medieval village that achieved wealth from wool in 15th & 16th centuries   **295**

296 Bodiam Castle, East Sussex: built in 1385 to defend against a French invasion that never came

Raglan Castle, Monmouthshire, Wales: built in 1435

Herstmonceux Castle, East Sussex: built in 1441 on the site of an old manor house

St Catherines Chapel, Abbotsbury, Dorset: built in 1400 as a pilgrim chapel

300 Glamis Castle, Angus, Scotland: the childhood home of the Queen Mother, built in 14th century

Sinclair and Girnigoe Castle, Caithness, Scotland: dates back to late 15th century

Medieval open fields at Laxton, Nottinghamshire

Appleton-le-Moors, Yorkshire: a village that has preserved its medieval layout 303

304   Medieval strip lynchets near Uploders, Dorset

Medieval fields in Swaledale near Crackpot, North Yorkshire

Deal Castle, Kent: a Device Fort built by Henry VIII in 1539

REFORMATION AND REVOLUTION

1485 - 1660

The Weald, that great swathe of land – much of it still densely wooded today – stretching from Kent across East and West Sussex and into Surrey, was the setting for an industry in the sixteenth and seventeenth centuries that symbolized some of the huge changes – political, social, economic and military – that occurred between 1500 and 1660. During this time the country was transformed from a medieval to a recognizably modern state, and one on the way to becoming a world power. The geology of the Weald harboured quantities of iron ore and this, combined with charcoal from the coppiced woodlands, together with the streams providing motive power, proved the ideal setting for an iron industry. Many places, from Asburnham, Heathfield and Robertsbridge in Kent to Abinger Hammer, Gomshall and Shere in Surrey, rang to the sound of the iron masters' hammers as iron was forged not only for domestic use – such as fire backs, water pipes, pots and pans – but also for cannon. Improbable as it may seem to anyone enjoying these quiet woods now, the Weald was the centre of an armaments industry that, from 1525, included gunpowder manufacture at Chilworth in Surrey.

The breakdown of the feudal system that paved the way for a more flexible labour market coincided with a dynastic change in the monarchy. The victor of Bosworth, Henry VII, cautious and prudent, managed to withstand a serious challenge to his position from a rebellion led by Perkin Warbeck. He married his daughter to the Scottish king, thus ensuring peace of his northern border during his reign. He also built a vast fortune, and by the time he died in 1509 the dynasty was secure, and the throne passed peacefully to his free-spending son Henry VIII spent money on display and warfare. Some military expeditions were defensive, such as that to repel a Scottish invasion at the battle of Flodden Field in 1513. Others, such as the campaigns in France the same year, were aggressive and vastly expensive. Artillery warfare, a new type of warfare, with gunpowder and cannon replacing the medieval longbows, eventually made the massive Norman castles obsolete. In 1538 the country was threatened with invasion by France and Spain, and Henry began a huge defensive programme involving the construction of artillery fortresses along the south coast, from the Thames to Dorset. These were essentially heavily reinforced gun platforms accommodating trained gunners; some such as Deal and Walmer still survive, although the invasion never materialized.

Henry's obsessive anxiety about his lack of a male heir, coupled with his need for money, was to bring about two enormous changes which impacted profoundly on the people, their communities and the landscape. When Henry came to the throne, the centre of most communities – whether in town or countryside – was the parish church, often the only public building, so not only the focus of religious devotion but also the social hub of the community. The rites of passage were carried out in the church and the calendar of the church year was filled with feasts, fasts and ritual, around which the lives of the parishioners revolved. Some practices, such as the plough festivities occurring in January, were essentially pagan fertility rites that had been absorbed into the Christian calendar. The spiritual lord of the church was the pope, far away in Rome, and it was the pope's refusal to grant Henry an annulment of his first marriage to the Spanish princess, Catherine of Aragon, which had failed to produce a male heir, that resulted in the break with Rome, and Henry's declaration of himself as head of the church in 1534. This separation, the political genesis of the English Reformation, was to pave the way for fundamental religious shift as England changed from being a Roman Catholic to a Protestant country.

Henry was also responsible for an enormous land grab – nothing less than the redistribution of the wealth of the monasteries. Monasticism as a way of life was in decline by this date, and Henry was quick to see that, as head of the church, the monasteries of England and Wales were his for the taking to enrich the royal coffers. By 1539 all had surrendered, and the charitable functions of caring for the sick and aiding the poor had disappeared with them. Their lands were sold, the former monastic buildings either lying derelict to be plundered for their lead and stone, or else being rebuilt as grand houses – Audley End in Essex for example – at the centres of the new estates. Some abbey churches – such as Peterborough – became cathedrals, while others, such as Rievaulx, Jervaulx and Fountains remain in their remote ruined splendour. In Scotland the process was slower and less clear-cut but the decline was irreversible, and by 1587 all monastic property had been annexed to the Scottish crown.

Despite the dynastic links, Scotland had maintained its independence while Wales, with only a population of some 250,000, was now governed directly from England. During Henry's reign the population of England began to increase sharply, almost doubling in size to more than four million by the end of the sixteenth century. The reason for this was probably a combination of circumstances, including a reduction in disease and higher fertility rates. But improved fertility eluded Henry and, despite his six wives, he produced only one legitimate son, Edward VI, together with two daughters, Mary and Elizabeth.

During Edward's brief reign, the political Reformation began to bite in terms of religious practice, with a series of laws proscribing how people worshipped. The power of the state to interfere in the church became brutally apparent when the parish churches were robbed of their ornaments – the treasures of past generations – which meant the wholesale destruction of medieval works of art. The interiors of the churches were stripped out: their wall paintings, designed to instruct an illiterate population, whitewashed over; their carvings smashed or removed; the vestments, gold and silver taken away. The church calendar was revised and many of the old customs, such as the plough celebrations, banned. In short, the state dictated what went on in the places that had been central to the life of communities for generations. Unlike her profoundly Catholic sister, Mary I, the Protestant Elizabeth I managed to steer a course between the extremes of the reformers and the more conservative elements. An extreme Protestant group known as the Puritans became a significant force during her long reign (1558-1603). In Scotland, John Knox was spreading the religious teachings of the French theologian, John Calvin; for many in England the certainties Calvinism offered an attractive alternative to the unsettling hybrid of the politically inspired reformation.

The Spanish attempted invasion in 1588 but were defeated by a combination of the English navy under Sir Francis Drake and adverse weather. The fortifications in the Isles of Scilly bear witness to the military preoccupations of those years, as do the walls at Berwick-upon-Tweed just south of the Scottish border. The need to build ships and the increasing population put Britain's forests under pressure with large-scale forest clearance. The Tudor dynasty ended in 1603 with the death of Elizabeth. Her kinsman, James VI of Scotland inherited her throne, thus uniting the two crowns of Scotland and England.

But the later sixteenth and seventeenth centuries were nevertheless a period of growth and exploration. Spain and Portugal were establishing settlements in the Americas, and the trade across the Atlantic between the Old and the New World was a harbinger of the future with three countries – France, Spain and England – vying with each other for commercial and naval dominance. As a maritime country, with plenty of harbours, England was well placed to take advantage of new opportunities, and English merchants went east and west in search of trade. Conspicuous

nsumption was evident in the great houses built by the wealthiest Elizabethans and Jacobeans, houses that were
o longer fortified. Hardwick Hall in Derbyshire, Charlton House at Greenwich, Hatfield House in Hertfordshire
nd Castle Ashby in Northamptonshire epitomize the new, confident architecture. This confidence is also reflected
town houses, such as Ireland's Mansion in Shrewbury, Shropshire, and manor houses – Penarth at Newtown
Powys, and Wraxall in Dorset. Public buildings also became more common – for example the Town House at
ulross in Fife, the administrative centre of the town, and the market hall at Ledbury. Artistic and cultural horizons
ere also expanding – this was the age of Shakespeare and the Globe Theatre.

he great population explosion meant more mouths to feed at a time when a series of bad harvests in the 1590s
ought hunger and the prospect of unrest. The amount of agricultural land in production needed to be increased by
leasing land from the royal forests and ploughing up the waste and common land. But there were vested interests
work, from the cottagers who would lose the right to pasture their animals if land were enclosed, through the
nks of the landowners to the king, who was reluctant to lose potential income from crown land. In Scotland, with
e population dependent on subsistence farming, a famine in 1623 took a heavy toll. The opening up of colonies in
aces such as Virginia and New England attracted many migrants keen to find better lives elsewhere – an estimated
ird of a million people left Britain in the seventeenth century. James's son, Charles I, was inadequate to the task
steering either England or Scotland through a period of unrest and change. Rather, he aggravated the situation,
enating the Scots by trying to force on them the English prayer book, interfering in matters of landownership and
ming into conflict with Parliament, believing he could rule England without it.

e consequence was the Civil War, which began in 1642 between Charles and the Royalist forces on one side
d Parliamentary forces on the other. The Scots first backed the English Parliamentarians and military defeat of
e Royalists ended with Charles' capture and public execution at Whitehall in 1649. Fighting extended across the
untry, the roll call of battles including Edgehill in 1642, Marston Moor in 1644, Naseby in 1645, Preston in 1648,
unbar in 1650 and Worcester in 1651. The royalist defeat at Worcester sent Charles' son and heir – the future
harles II – who was then backed by the Scots, into exile for nine years. England became a military state under the
iritan leader of the Parliamentary forces, Oliver Cromwell, who brought Scotland under direct English rule for the
st time. His death in 1658 paved the way for the restoration of the monarchy in 1660, to a country which by then
d tired of the restrictions of Puritan rule.

e Civil War was a highly divisive conflict, splitting communities and families. An example of the ferocity with
nich it was fought can be seen in the broken-backed silhouette of Corfe Castle in Dorset, which was twice besieged
Parliamentary troops in 1643 and 1645 before it eventually fell. It was 'slighted', that is rendered useless as a
tress. Raglan Castle in Monmouthshire, the stronghold of the Earl of Worcester, was destroyed after an eleven-
ek siege. Basing House in Hampshire had been rebuilt as a huge palace in 1535 – the largest private house in
gland – on the site of an old castle. Under John Paulet, the Marquess of Winchester, it became a centre for Royalist
d Catholic sympathisers, until Cromwell's soldiers efficiently reduced it to a smoking ruin.

arles II returned to a country that was weary of war, and he effectively drew a line under the events of the previous
ven years by granting a pardon to those who would pledge him loyalty, with the exception of those involved in the
ath of his father. King and parliament were restored, but not as before. The absolute power of the monarch was
moved: the future balance of power was to be in the hands of parliament rather than those of the sovereign.

Oxburgh Hall, Norfolk: a 15th-century moated manor house

Compton Wynyates, Warwickshire: a Tudor period country house, built in 15th century

312 Drummond Castle, Scotland: a late 15th century castle and 17th century Scottish Renaissance gar

…ughty Castle, Dundee, Scotland: built in 15th century to protect the Tay estuary, now a museum **313**

Blickling Hall, Norfolk: originally a 15th century stately home, rebuilt in 17th century

Basing House, Hampshire: a 16th century Tudor palace

Chatsworth House, Derbyshire: a 17th century country house

Little Moreton Hall, Cheshire

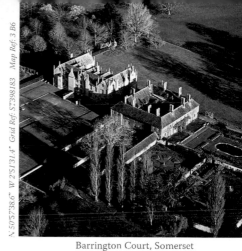

Barrington Court, Somerset

N 50°57'38.6" W 2°51'31.4" Grid Ref: ST398183   Map Ref: 3 B6

Kentwell Hall, Suffolk

Burghley House, Lincolnshire

N 52°38'32.7" W 0°27'09.2" Grid Ref: TF048061   Map Ref: 7 A5

Mary Rose Dock, Portsmouth, Hampshire: where the Tudor warship, the 'Mary Rose' is housed

Chatham Historic Dockyard, Kent: a Royal Dockyard in 1613-1984, now a maritime museum

Montacute House, Somerset: a 16th century Elizabethan country house

Hurst Castle, Hampshire: a Device Fort built by Henry VIII in 1541

322 St Catherines Castle, Fowey, Cornwall: built by Henry VIII in 16th century to protect Fowey harb

Lindisfarne Castle, Northumberland

N 58°38'50.7" W 3°13'29.2" Grid Ref: ND290739 Map Ref: 15 G2

Castle of Mey, Caithness, Scotland

Upnor Castle, Kent

N 51°12'02.0" E 1°24'07.0" Grid Ref: TR278501 Map Ref: 4 M7

Walmer Castle, Kent

324   Exeter Canal, Devon: built in 1563, one of the oldest artificial waterways in the UK

Afon Garreg Wen sheepfold, Snowdonia, North Wales: 17th century multi-cellular sheepfold **325**

326 Longleat House, Somerset: 16th century country house, a fine example of Elizabethan architect[...]

Hardwick Hall, Derbyshire

N 52°01'14.8" E 0°13'14.9" Grid Ref: TL525381 Map Ref: 7 E14

Audley End House, Essex

Hatfield House, Hertfordshire

N 52°54'26.5" E 1°15'34.3" Grid Ref: TG193394 Map Ref: 7 I6

Felbrigg Hall, Norfolk

Longford Castle, near Salisbury, Wiltshire: built in the late 16th century

Thirlestane Castle, Borders, Scotland: dates back to 13th century, present building is 16th century **329**

330 Globe Theatre: a replica of the original Globe Theatre of Shakespeare fame, which opened in 159

Cerne Abbas Giant, Dorset: records go back to 17th century but it is possibly Iron Age in origin

332 Iron Bridge, Shropshire: cradle of the Industrial Revolution and the famous iron bridge built in 1

FROM FARM TO FACTORY

1660 - 1901

muel Pepys was a close observer of Restoration London. His diary, which runs from 1 January 1660 to 31 May 69, gives a vivid picture of the city in the years during the last great outbreak of plague in 1665, and the devastation ought by the fire the following year. It also provides a unique insight into the career of a successful professional an, a civil servant whose administrative genius helped to shape the British navy, at a time when the country was the verge of great change and development. This was an age when interest in scientific study and thought was owing: the Royal Society – the oldest and most important scientific society – was founded officially in 1660, ceiving in 1662 a royal charter to publish its findings. The new king, Charles II, approved of science and art, as ll as women. The gaiety and lively behaviour of his court were in sharp contrast to the dour conditions of the ommonwealth, where even the theatre had been banned.

t whereas in previous centuries the role of the monarch had been pivotal in the fortunes of Britain, the emphasis the eighteen and nineteenth centuries is on the mercantile wealth created by overseas trade and the agricultural d industrial revolutions at home. London was now by far the largest city in Britain; by 1700, its population had own to some half a million people, 10 per cent of the entire population of England and Wales. But, in the late venteenth century, Britain was still overwhelmingly an agrarian country, with the lottery of location dictating e relative poverty or wealth of its inhabitants. Life in the Scottish Highlands, with its low soil fertility and short owing season required particular endurance. Cattle droving flourished: animals were brought down from the ghlands into towns such as Falkirk or Crieff, sold on by the drovers, then fattened on the good grassland of rthumberland and Yorkshire before beginning the long journey south to the markets there. Transhumance – the actice of moving sheep and cattle to higher summer pastures – occurred in the highland areas of both Scotland d Wales, continuing in the more remote locations until the nineteenth century. A series of poor harvests in otland in the 1690s caused severe hardship. The population there is estimated to have reached a million only in early years of the eighteenth century.

me of the provincial towns of England were thriving trade centres at this period, and many had developed cialist trades – the association of place and product such as Witney blankets and Kidderminster carpets still onating today. The social unit was centred round the partnership of husband and wife; for many this was also economic partnership. In towns, small tradesmen and their wives tended to work together. Some women ran ir own businesses such as alehouses, but in general, small businesses – bakers and brewers for example – would olve both partners. Men overwhelmingly dominated in the crafts; apprenticeships for girls were very few in mparison to those available for boys.

the small yeoman farmer, the work of his wife – whose responsibilities traditionally included the dairy, feeding ltry and pigs as well as the care of the house, garden and children – was indispensable. A woman would take n to the mill for grinding, or travel to market to sell produce, as well as to buy those things not manufactured on farm. At times, her labour was needed in the fields, behind the plough or helping with the harvest. The woman ose husband left home each day to work another's land would keep the house and garden in her husband's ence, as well as tend any smallholding.

Agricultural methods in many parts of Britain were essentially the same as they had been in the Middle Ages, a
were inadequate to feed an increasing population. A new, more technological approach to land management a
crop production was necessary – in effect an agricultural revolution that was an integral part of the industr
revolution which transformed the country into a manufacturing and urban society. This involved both releasing la
for agriculture and devising methods of improving crop yields, the better to sustain both man and beast. This h
started in the early 1600s when water meadows, the irrigation of which could be controlled according to requireme
were developed in places such as the area between Salisbury and Downton in southern England. Good graz
enabled more animals to be overwintered and their manure to enrich the ground. These were expensive proje
though, and other methods of getting the most from the land were developing. In the Midlands in particular,
method of maintaining permanent grassland and cultivated land was abandoned in favour of an alternating system
seven years of cultivation followed by seeding the land to become a grass ley, or meadow, for up to 12 years. For
first time, turnips were grown in Suffolk on a large-scale, and interest in specialist cattle and sheep breeding grew

Providing more land for agricultural development had been going on in England through the process of enclos
– creating hedged or ditched fields – since the fourteenth century. This had meant the loss of common land
grazing and wood gathering, causing distress to the more vulnerable in the rural economy. The process was hug
accelerated in the eighteenth century by the so-called 'Parliamentary enclosures' where the landowners bought
great tracts of common land, open fields and woodland pastures, which they then rented out. During the reign
George III (1760-1820) an estimated two million hectares of land were enclosed. An example of this can be s
today at Leckhampstead in Buckinghamshire.

The other way of increasing agricultural land was through drainage. A Dutch engineer, Cornelius Vermuyden,
responsible for a massive reclamation project in Bedfordshire, Cambridgeshire and Norfolk in the seventee
century, thus creating more than 200,000 hectares of land. The marshes at Romney in Kent were drained to gr
sheep. Agriculture was fast becoming an industry, the great landowners, controlling vast acreages through t
estates. The Dukes of Buccleuch and Devonshire, for example, owned extensive estates in the south of Scotland
Northamptonshire, and Derbyshire, respectively. Great houses were built such as Ickworth House in Suffolk
many more modest country residences. It was an age of building expansion. The planned development of Edinbu
New Town was built to accommodate the growing city, a series of crescents and squares with a grid of stre
that stretched away elegantly from the old medieval centre. The symmetry and design of both Edinburgh and B
another planned Georgian development, can best be appreciated from the air. Similarly distinctive rows of terra
homes were constructed in many of Britain's towns and cities. London developed westwards, first eating up
around Covent Garden, St James's and Bloomsbury.

If the varied geology of Britain required innovation to increase its agricultural potential, it also held the raw mate
that was literally the fuel for the Industrial Revolution – a period generally defined as lasting between 1750 and 1
The first iron bridge in the world at Ironbridge Gorge is a lasting symbol of the emerging technology. The coalfi
of Scotland, the north-east of England, North and South Wales and the North Midlands provided the motive po
for the world's first large-scale industrialization. The harnessing of steam power and the development of a pum
engine was essential to the growth of the mining industry – tin, lead and especially coal. The slate mines of W
and the deposits of brick clay in southern and central England, provided the raw material of the houses needed fo
ever-expanding urban population. A combination of technological advance – the invention of machines that c

the work of spinning and weaving on a far greater scale and at a faster speed than any human being could – and an ...anding labour force from the increasing population, took the textile industry out of the homes of the cottagers and ... the factories. Heavy industry developed and new towns – such as Birmingham, Manchester and Leeds – grew up ...ere once there had been villages. The port of Liverpool in the north-west expanded with a huge dock construction ...gramme in the 1840s.

...e social impact was to draw people off the land and into the cities, creating a large urban working-class. By the time ...toria succeeded to the throne in 1837, the links with the land as a way of life were rapidly weakening. The price ...ndustrialization was high, paid not just in environmental degradation, but critically and cruelly with the lives and ...lth of thousands of men, women and children who laboured in the mines, factories and mills. The conditions were ...n appalling: children worked underground in the mines, and the first factory acts included legislation limiting ...ir working hours. In the crowded industrial cities with their inadequate sanitation, disease flourished.

...mmunications too were changing. Initially the canal system, dug with spade and shovel, was designed to carry ...e quantities of raw material across the whole country, and there was a boom in waterway construction towards ... end of the eighteenth century. Associated now with leisurely narrowboat journeys, the canal network with its ...em of locks, such as the Caen Hill locks on the Kennet and Avon Canal, linked the country in a way that was ...nown since Roman times. The Forth and Clyde canal joined Edinburgh with Glasgow, the Shropshire Union canal ...etrated as far as Welshpool, and the Grand Union struck northwards from London to Northamptonshire, to name ... a few. The coming of the railways redefined and shaped the landscape in yet another way, taking over the role of ...waterways. Between 1860 and 1890, the rail network was put in place so that all the major towns and cities, and ...t of the smaller ones, were accessible by train.

... travel was not confined to the wealthy; anyone who could afford the third-class fare travelled by train. The age ...e commuter, the worker who travelled daily from one place to work in another, had arrived and the needs of the ...muter were met by the creation of suburbs. By the mid-nineteenth century the population of England alone had ...hed almost 17 million, and was to nearly double again by 1900. The expansion of London into the counties of ...dlesex, Surrey, Essex and Kent meant the destruction of many rural communities, as the land between the old ...ges was built over. Farms and market gardens disappeared beneath a covering of brick terraces and villas – the ...way suburbs   constructed to house the workforce of the capital. Whether factory worker, civil servant, clerk, ...der, docker or shopkeeper, all needed to be housed and so the suburbs grew, ringing London and other major ...n centres.

...don was also the hub of a much larger economic and political system that had developed over the previous 150 ...s, and which impacted on millions of people around the world. By 1900, the British Empire had extended across ...globe to include many countries such as present-day India, Pakistan, Burma, Sri Lanka, Jamaica, Trinidad and ...ago, Ghana and Nigeria, Australia and Canada. British trading prosperity had also come at a very high price, being ...ely bound up with the slave trade until it became illegal in 1807. The ships that took the enslaved men and women ... Africa to work plantations in the West Indies returned to Britain with the product of their enforced labour ...tton, tobacco and sugar. By 1900, Britain depended on her huge merchant fleet. This imported food and raw ...erials from the colonies and exported manufactured goods worldwide, while her navy maintained her dominance ...a. But it was not set to last: almost as quickly as it came, Britain's economic and industrial strength was to wane.

St Paul's Cathedral, London: built in 17th century, on the site of a Saxon cathedral

Houghton Hall, Norfolk: a 18th century country house, a fine example of Palladian architecture   **337**

338   Blenheim Palace, Oxfordshire: one of England's largest houses, built in early 18th century

orth House, Suffolk: a 18th century country house, a neoclassical structure with a giant rotunda

340   Levant Tin & Copper Mine, Cornwall: 19th century, featuring a working beam engine

Gwennap Pit, Cornwall: created by a mining subsidence in 18th century, now an amphitheatre **341**

342 Fort George, Scotland: a massive fortress built in 18th century and still in use as army barracks

rt Tregantle, Cornwall: completed in 1865 to guard against the French landings at Whitesand Bay **343**

344   Bath, Somerset: The Royal Crescent is a fine example of 18th century Georgian architecture

Eastnor Castle, Herefordshire: a 19th century mock castle

City of London, with many Georgian buildings

British Museum, London

N 51°30'38.4" W 0°07'01.1" Grid Ref: TQ308808 Map Ref: 17 G7

Somerset House, London

Bank of England, London

N 51°30'11.7" W 0°07'32.7" Grid Ref: TQ301799 Map Ref: 17 G8

Downing Street, London

Sovereign Harbour, Eastbourne, East Sussex, with a 19th century Martello Tower

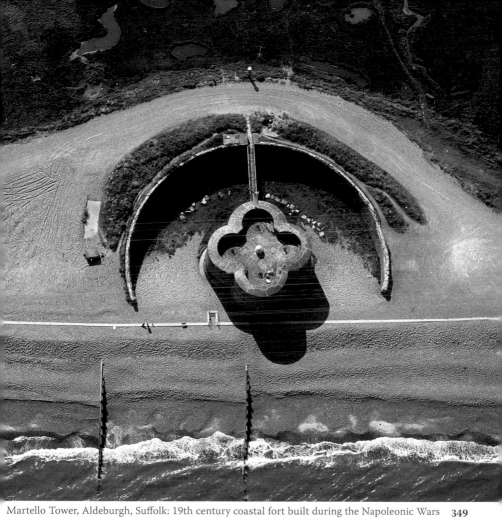

Martello Tower, Aldeburgh, Suffolk: 19th century coastal fort built during the Napoleonic Wars **349**

350 Trafalgar Square, London: completed in 1845 to commemorate the Battle of Trafalgar in 1805

St Katherine Docks, London: opened as a dock in 1828 and now a marina

Highclere Castle, Berkshire: a Victorian country house, built in 1838 to 1842

354   Rhondda Heritage Park, Trehafod, Rhondda Valley, South Wales: a partially preserved coalmine

Stobswood opencast coalmine, near Morpeth, Northumberland

356 Mormond White Horse, Aberdeenshire: most northerly horse hill figure in Britain, created in 18

Jack and Gill Windmills, Clayton, West Sussex: date back to 1850s

358 China Clay quarries, near St Austell, Cornwall.: China clay has been quarried here for 200 years

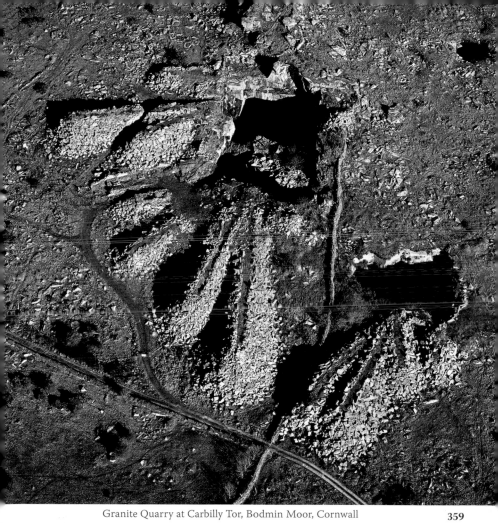

Granite Quarry at Carbilly Tor, Bodmin Moor, Cornwall

Crewe Railway Yards, Cheshire: opened in 1837 and rebuilt in 1861

Liverpool Waterfront, Merseyside

362 Gladstone Pottery, Longton, Stoke-on-Trent, Staffordshire: opened in 1787, now a museum

Royton, near Rochdale, Greater Manchester: 19th century textile mills

364 Leckhampstead, Buckinghamshire: Ridge and Furrow crossed by Parliamentary field enclosures

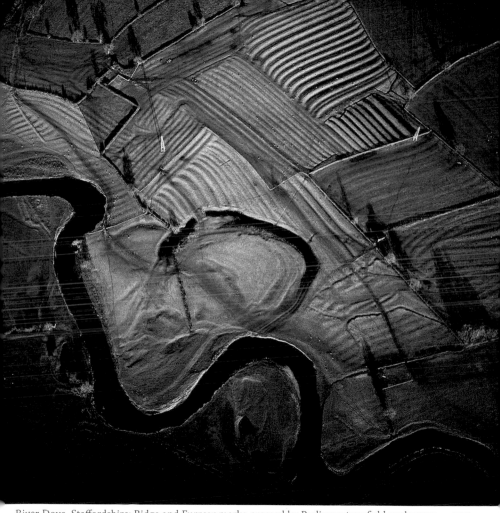

River Dove, Staffordshire: Ridge and Furrow marks crossed by Parliamentary field enclosures   **365**

366   Buckingham Palace: became the official royal palace of the British monarch in 1837

Houses of Parliament, Big Ben, & Westminster Abbey, London

Balmoral Castle, Aberdeenshire, Scotland: became a royal residence in 1848

Harlaxton Manor, Lincolnshire

N 58°12'40.2" W 6°23'43.2" Grid Ref: NB419331 Map Ref: 4 E10

Lews Castle, Stornoway, Lewis, Scotland

Victoria and Albert Museum, London

N 51°29'45.8" W 0°10'35.1" Grid Ref: TQ267790 Map Ref: 7 E8

Natural History Museum, London

Waterloo Train Station, London: opened in 1848

Tower Bridge, London: opened in 1894

372   ICI Winnington Works, Northwich, Cheshire: established in 1873

Brickworks at Whittlesea, near Peterborough, Cambridgeshire

374   Arten Gill Railway Viaduct, Yorkshire, on the Settle-Carlisle railway constructed in 1870

Forth Bridges, Edinburgh: the railway bridge and road bridge cross the Firth of Forth

Palace Pier, Brighton, East Sussex, was opened in 1899

Manchester Ship Canal: opened in 1894, transformed Manchester to a major sea port

378 Canary Wharf, London: built on the site of the West India Docks, the development starting in 19

MODERN BRITAIN

The landscape of Britain has probably changed more in the last century than in the previous two millennia. The opening years of the twentieth century gave little hint of what was to follow: two devastating wars (1914-1918 and 1939-1945), the second of which was to bankrupt the country, and a series of social, economic and technological changes that would transform radically how people lived, as well as the country they inhabited.

The first years were quiet enough. Queen Victoria died in 1901 and was succeeded by her son, Edward, and then her grandson George in 1910. Motor cars were appearing on the roads and Britain still retained her place in the front rank as a manufacturing and trading nation. However, women did not have the vote, and it was only in 1928 that they were given voting rights on the same basis as men. But on 4 August 1914 Britain declared war on Germany the consequence of imperial rivalries between Germany and Austro-Hungary on the one side, and France, Britain and Russia on the other. The empires controlled by the European powers at the time meant that the conflict and its effects were widespread, affecting people across the globe – this was the First World War. Men enlisted from across the Empire, 1.5 million from India alone. In Europe it was a war of stalemate and trench warfare, which saw the use of poison gas and the introduction of the tank. Conscription was introduced in Britain in 1916, and as men left their jobs women stepped forward to replace them, working in industry as well as on the land. Britain's dependence on imported food was clearly demonstrated when supplies were severely disrupted by German submarines, and rationing was introduced in 1918, despite a bumper harvest the previous year. The casualties of war were enormous, the dead being commemorated on thousands of war memorials across Britain, including one for Indian soldiers on the South Downs above Brighton. Almost nine million men were mobilized from the Empire, of whom more than 10,000 were killed and more than two million wounded, with nearly 200,000 listed as prisoners or missing. Hard on the heels of war came the flu pandemic of 1918-9. In Britain alone more 250,000 people died, wartime conditions contributing to the death toll.

In 1918, much of the housing stock of Britain was of poor quality, with many people living in grimy crowded terraces and tenements of the cities and suburbs built with little or no regard to the health and welfare of the inhabitants. The concept of the garden city had already been put forward by Ebenezer Howard, who believed that towns should be carefully planned, of limited size and incorporate the best elements of both town and country. His ideas led to the building of Letchworth Garden City and Welwyn Garden City, both in Hertfordshire.

An increased demand for housing, as well as the desire of many to leave the crowded environment of the cities in favour of what was perceived to be a more pastoral existence, resulted in the massive expansion of suburbs, especially around London. Much agricultural and horticultural land was consumed in the interwar years. The Second World War effectively put a halt to this uncontrolled growth, but by then a huge area around London reaching into Kent, Middlesex, Surrey, Hertfordshire and Essex had been covered with row after row of mostly semi-detached houses, each with a front and back garden within which to recreate the pastoral idyll. Glasgow and Birmingham also both grew rapidly during this period, the former more than doubling in size between 1926 and 1938. There was little regard for traditional regional building materials and styles, but many of these houses had a new and innovative feature that heralded the future – a garage for a private motor car. It was Britain's increasing preference for motor transport that was to impact most heavily on the landscape, and on the quality of life, in the twentieth century.

Private car ownership had reached almost two million just before the Second World War, with half a million good and freight vehicles on the road. The Ministry of Transport was established in 1919, and set about devising a system of classification for roads.

But for many families the experience of the interwar years was that of hardship, as economic depression and industrial slow-down created high unemployment. One road-building scheme set up in part to provide work for the unemployed was the Trunk Road Programme, responsible for a network of roads which went round – by-passes – rather than through towns. At the beginning of the century, road surfaces were either dirt tracks, or else were composed of a hard-core of stone topped by rubble, mortar and clay – a method devised by a Scottish engineer, John McAdam, nearly a century earlier. A more durable and less dusty road surface was needed for motor transport and the development of 'tarmac', where bitumen was used to bind and seal the surface, solved the problem. This in turn opened up areas of the country that hitherto had been effectively cut off for want of a good road. It also meant that as roads were built, ribbon development occurred alongside, as can be seen on the Kingston bypass near London.

The First World War had jump-started the development of aviation in Britain while the post-war period saw its growth into a commercial industry. The grass fields of some of the wartime airstrips were developed into civilian airports. London's airport at this time was at Croydon. Heston in Middlesex was opened in 1929, but plans develop it as a major alternative to Croydon were halted by the outbreak of war. The land on which Heathrow was to develop was first acquired in 1929 and was used mainly for test flying. Manchester was the location for the first scheduled air service in 1919 with planes flying from Alexandra Park airfield. In 1930 Manchester Airport opened at Barton, although this was to be replaced by one at Ringway.

The industrial recession was also mirrored by an agricultural depression. In many villages there was a sharp decline in population, with land going out of production. Attempts to reverse the trend were made, such as the smallholding movement whereby local councils made parcels of land available to agricultural labourers; this reached its peak the mid-1920s with 30,000 smallholdings in England and Wales. The Forestry Commission, created in 1919 to deal with the timber shortages of the war, covered large areas of land in Scotland, Wales and northern England with conifer plantations. On the eve of war in 1939, Britain was still importing 70 per cent of its food.

The six years of the Second World War impacted much more heavily on the civilian population than the First, with large-scale aerial bombardment. The City and the East End of London were especially badly hit. Overall, an estimated 110,000 houses were destroyed in London, with nearly 300,000 more suffering serious damage. Enemy bombers ranged over the country targeting major ports and industrial areas including Swansea, Cardiff, Glasgow, Bristol, Manchester, Liverpool and Birmingham. The medieval centres of Coventry and Southampton were flattened. order to feed the country, huge areas of land were once again put under the plough. The Women's Land Army play a vital role in these war years, not only in agriculture but also in forestry. Food rationing was imposed in 1940 and was not to be withdrawn completely until 1954. With an invasion expected, coastal defences were put in place, some of which can still be seen, such as at Portishead and around the approaches to Scapa Flow. Numerous pillboxes can still be found, as can the remains of some of the many airfields, such as those at Alconbury in Cambridgeshire and Waddington in Lincolnshire. RAF Duxford in Cambridgeshire is now part of the Imperial War Museum. Tyneham village in Dorset was taken over by the army, a war-time requisition that proved to be permanent.

The post-war years altered the face of Britain radically. In one way they can be seen as a repetition of the interwar years, but on a very different scale. The pressing need for housing meant that thousands of new homes had to be built. New towns were developed, initially as satellites to London in places such as Basildon, Harlow and Stevenage, and then elsewhere in Britain including Corby, Milton Keynes, Telford, Runcorn, Washington and Warrington. Tower blocks replaced the old tenement blocks of Glasgow, echoing those built for the huge council estate at Roehampton in south-west London.

Heavy industry – including shipbuilding and coal mining – declined to the point of invisibility, and the economic base of Britain changed to that of a service economy. The railways never properly recovered from the damage inflicted on them during the Second World War, and they received a near-fatal blow with the closure of many branch lines in the 1960s, reducing the network by a third to some 12,000 miles. The Channel Tunnel – opened in 1994 – led to the first new railway construction for more than fifty years. The post-war increase in private car ownership has given the car priority in road and town planning: out of town retail developments, motorways, road widening schemes and housing estates springing up across the country irrespective of any public transport links, are all testament to the dominance of the internal combustion engine. There are now more than 30 million cars on Britain's roads.

The huge increase in road transport has been mirrored by that in the air. Heathrow was taken over by the Ministry of Civil Aviation in 1946. It had one runway and an army surplus tent did duty as an airport building. In the early 1950s, the tent gave way to the first terminal building – now Terminal 2. By 1986 there were two runways to accommodate aircraft and four terminals, and a fifth terminal was opened in 2008. Plans for a third runway, seen as vital to the airport's future, would involve the demolition of much of nearby Harmondsworth. In 2006, a total of more than 225 million passengers were processed through Britain's airports.

The total population of the United Kingdom now exceeds 60 million, with those of Scotland and Wales numbering some five million and three million people respectively, people whose way and quality of life is almost totally dependent on high technology, fuelled by power stations such as Fiddlers Ferry near Warrington and Calder Hall in Cumbria. Huge oil refineries at places such as Milford Haven in Wales help to keep the country moving. Oil platforms, such as Beatrice in the North Sea, exploit natural resources laid down in the far geological past. Nature can also wreak havoc, as shown by the 2007 floods across large parts of country, including Gloucestershire, while London, now one of the world's leading financial markets, is reliant on the Thames Barrier to keep its feet dry.

Post-war Britain has had to adapt to meet a changing world. The union with Wales and Scotland has entered a new phase, with devolution and the establishment of the Scottish Parliament and the Welsh Assembly. Britain is no longer an imperial power – the former colonies and dominions have achieved independence – and is now part of the European Union alongside former rivals and enemies. But the legacy of previous generations is still visible: parts have become incorporated into the present fabric such as the regenerated London docklands, and the environmental themes of the Eden Project in a reclaimed china clay pit in Cornwall, while others, such as Stonehenge in Wiltshire and Hadrian's Wall in northern England, are acknowledged as monuments to be protected. Other parts of the legacy are more elusive and very vulnerable – the landscape of Britain itself – with its coastlines, hillsides, moors and heathlands, rivers, woods, hedgerows and fields. Whether, and for how long, these will survive is open to question.

382 Upton Towans national explosive works and storage depot, Cornwall, in operation 1888-1919

Howden Reservoir (1912), Peak District, Derbyshire

N 53°24'51.3" W 1°44'38.0" Grid Ref: SK171909 Map Ref: 9 B11

Angram (1919) & Scarhouse (1936) Reservoirs, Yorksh

N 51°04'12.8" E 0°23'39.2" Grid Ref: TQ678328 Map Ref: 4 G9

Bewl Water (1975), Kent and Sussex border

Roadford Reservoir (1988), Devon

Graffham Water, Cambridgeshire: opened in 1966

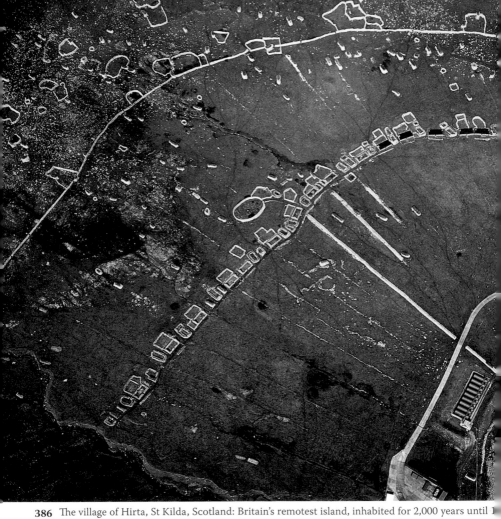

386 The village of Hirta, St Kilda, Scotland: Britain's remotest island, inhabited for 2,000 years until 1

Spade Cultivation, North Harris, Scotland: a cultivation method that did not change for centuries   **387**

388 The All England Lawn Tennis Club, Wimbledon: the first championships were held in 1877

Bristol Airport: a Second World War training airfield, now a growing hub for international travel **389**

390 Alconbury Airfield, Cambridgeshire: used by British and American air forces from 1938 to 1995

An underground tank farm at Redcliff Bay, Portishead, Somerset

392 Duxford Aerodrome, Cambridgeshire: Second World War fighter base, now a museum for aircraf

Sellafield , Cumbria: a nuclear power station that was originally an ordnance factory   **393**

394 Battersea Power Station, London: established in 1939 and ceased electricity-generation in 1983

West Burton Power Station, Nottinghamshire

396   Churchill Barriers at Scapa Flow, Orkney: built in the Second World War to deter German U-boa

Spaghetti Junction, Birmingham: opened in 1972

Sullom Voe Oil Terminal, Shetland

Beatrice Oil Platform, North Sea

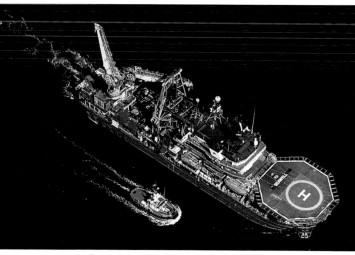

Oil rig service vessel, Lerwick, Shetland

Oil depot at Purfleet, Essex

Oil Refinery at Milford Haven, Pembrokeshire, South Wales

Morwenstow, Cornwall: satellite ground station

Thames Barrier, London: completed in 1984 to prevent surge tides from flooding London

M25/M23 Motorway Junction, Surrey: opened in 1976

Second Severn Bridge: opened in 1996, linking Monmouthshire with South Gloucestershire **405**

406 Canary Wharf, London: built on the site of the West India Docks, the development starting in 19

Channel Tunnel main terminal, near Folestone, Kent: opened in 1994

A cathedral of trees at Milton Keynes, Buckinghamshire

Murray Star Maze, a star-shaped hedge maze at Scone Palace, Perthshire, Scotland

Millennium Wheel or the 'London Eye', London: opened in 2000

Millennium Dome, London: built to celebrate the third millennium

412 Falkirk Wheel, Scotland: an ingenious device for lifting boats between canals, opened in 2002

30 St Mary Axe, known as "The Gherkin", London: a modern high rise building opened in 2004 **413**

414   Boscastle, Cornwall, was a scene of destruction in 2004 when flash floods hit the village.

Chartist Bridge, Blackwood, South Wales: a suspension bridge built in 2005   **415**

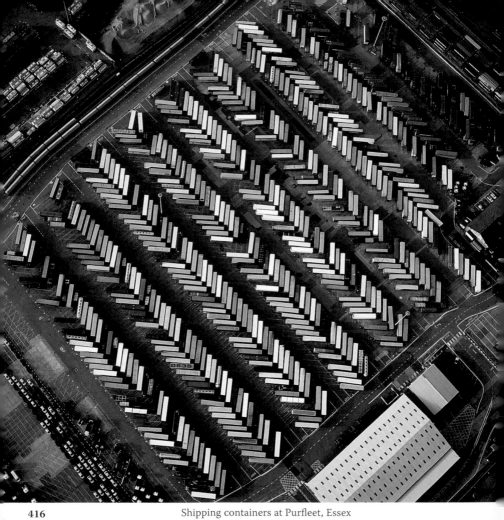

Shipping containers at Purfleet, Essex

Milton Keynes, Buckinghamshire: designer housing

Lincoln, Lincolnshire: terraced housing

Caravan park at Sandy Bay, near Exmouth, Devon

Farr Wind Farm, Glen Kyllachy, Tomatin, near Inverness, Scotland

Bush fire, Isle of Bute, Scotland

Pig farm, Wiltshire

Working fields, Wiltshire

424   Prawn farming, Isle of Lewis, Outer Hebrides, Scotland

Salmon farming, Shetland

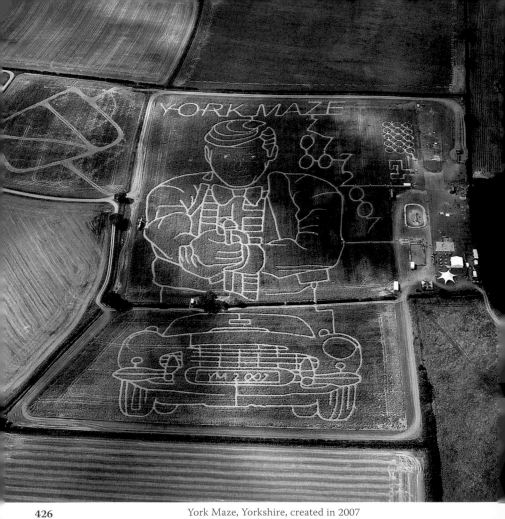

York Maze, Yorkshire, created in 2007

Crop Circle in preparation, near Avebury, Wiltshire

Floods at Tewkesbury, Gloucestershire, in 2007

Floods at Tirley, Gloucestershire, in 2007

Glastonbury Festival 2003, Pilton, Somerset

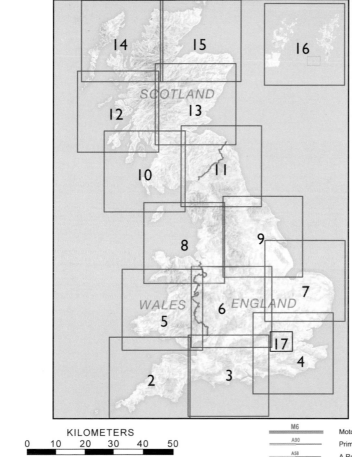

14
15
16
SCOTLAND
12
13
10
11
8
9
7
WALES
5
6
ENGLAND
17
4
2
3

KILOMETERS

| 0 | 10 | 20 | 30 | 40 | 50 |

MILES

| 0 | 10 | 20 | 30 | 40 | 50 |

M6 — Motorway
A90 — Primary Route Dual/Single
A58 — A Road Dual/Single
— Railway
■ Picture location

A B C D E F G H I J K L M

ISLES OF SCILLY

Tresco
St. Martin's
Bryher
Scilly Isles
Hugh Town
St. Mary's
St. Agnes

St. Just

Land's
End

Head
Swansea Bay
Pyle
Bridgend
M4
Porthcawl
Cowbridge

Nash Point
Bristol Chann

Foreland
Point
Lynmouth
Minehead

Lundy
Lundy Island
Ilfracombe
Combe
Martin
Cleeve Abbey

Woolacombe
Wimble
Barnstaple or
Bideford Bay
Braunton
Dulverton
Exebrid

Barnstaple
Northam
Hartland
Point
Bideford
Clovelly Dykes
South
Molton
Tiverton
Dyer's Lookout
Hartland
Great
Torrington
Chawleigh
Cullompton
Morwenstow
Chulmleigh
DEVON
Bude
Bay
Stratton
Holsworthy
Hatherleigh
Crediton
Exeter Cathedral
Bude
Roadford
Res
Okehampton
Exeter
Boscastle
Boscastle
Exeter Canal
Tintagel
Grimspound
Camelford
Launceston
Moretonhampstead
Houndtor
Sandy Bay
Colliford
Reserv
Carbilly Tor
Haytor Rocks
Padstow
Bronze age celtic fields
Wadebridge
Bodmin
Tavistock
Dunnabridge
and settlement
Pound
Newquay
Buckfastleigh
Liskeard
Torquay
CORNWALL
Restormel
Saltash
Buckfast Abbey
Castle
Totnes
Paignton
China Clay Quarries
Looe
Plymouth
St. Agnes
Fowey Polperro
Plympton
Brixham
St. Austell
Fort Tregantle
Ivybridge
Dartmouth
Chysauster
Upton
Mevagissey
St Catherine's
Kingsbridge
Start
Towans
Castle
Bay
Tregeseal
Gwennap
Whitsand
Salcombe
Circle
Bay
Carn
Merry Maidens
Penryn
Eigbury
Prawle
Euny
Stone Circle
St. Mawes
Bay
Point
Newlyn
Penzance
Falmouth
Land's
Boscawen-un
St Michael's Mount
Helston
Falmouth
End
Stone Circle
Bay
Mount's
Bay

Lizard
Lizard
Point

2

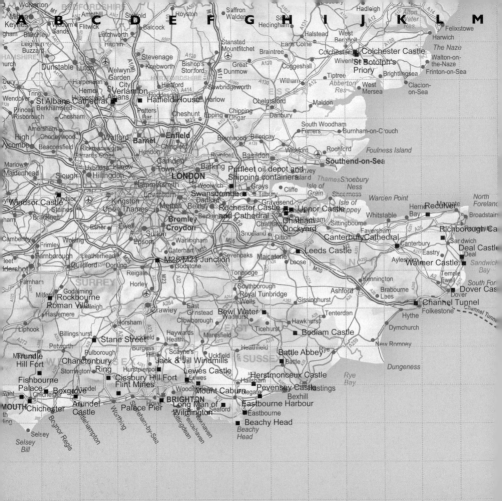

4

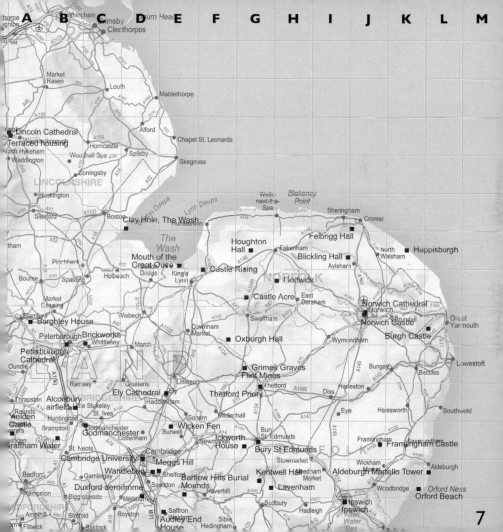

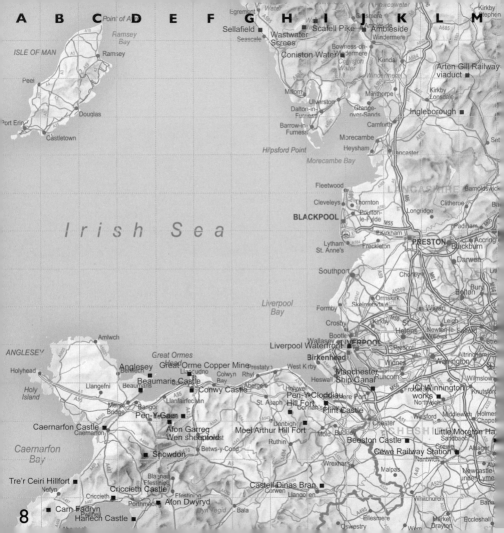

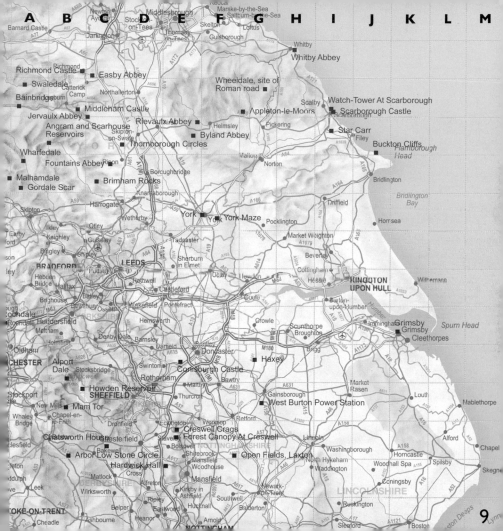

A B C D E F G H I J K L M

A B C D E F G H I J K L M

Daita
(Barraigh)

Eriskay

SEA OF THE HEBRIDES

Sandray
(Sanndraigh)

Pabbay
(Pabaigh)

Mingulay
(ughalaigh)

Canna

Rum

Snay

Cuillin Sound

Mallaig

Eigg

Sound of Rum

Muck

Sound of Eigg

Sound of Arisaig

INNER HEBRIDES

Coll

Tiree

Ardnamurchan
Volcanic Crater

Tioram Castle

Loch Shiel

Tobermory

Loch
Frisa

Sound of Mull

Loch Bà

MULL

Staffa - Fingal's Cave
and basalt columns

Ulva

Loch na Keal

Craignure

Connel

Oban

Duart Castle

Firth of Lorn

Iona

Iona

Scarba

Colonsay

Oronsay

JURA

Sound of Jura

Lochgilphead

Tarbert

ISLAY

Sound of Islay

Gigha

Sound of Gigha

Bush Fire

Bute

Tarbert

Rothesay
Great
Cumbrae

Millport

West
Kilbride

Ardrossan
Saltcoats

Broadford

Lochalsh

Sound of Sleat

Barrisdale Bay

Quoich

Loch
Nevis

Loch
Arkaig

Loch Morar

Loch
Garry

Loch
Lochy

Fort William

Ben Nevis

North
Ballachulish

Glencoe

Glaciated Valle
Glencoe

Loch Linnhe

Loch
Croran

Loch
Awe

Inveraray

Arr

Loch
Eck

Loch
Long

Helensbu

Dunoon

Gourok

Lan

Ki

Da

Sound of Bute

12

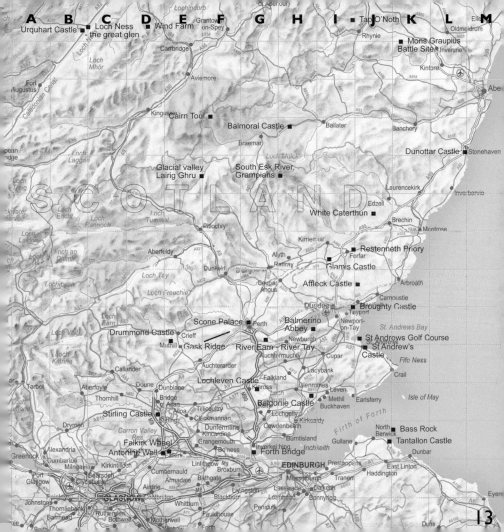

| A | B | C | D | E | F | G | H | I | J | K | L | M |

St Kilda
St Kilda

OUTER

Taransa
(Tarasaigh)

Toe
Head

Sound of Harris

Pabbay
Berneray

Cape Wra

Celler Head

HEBRIDES

OUTER

Isle of Lewis
(Eilean Leodhais)

Gallan
Head

Dun Carloway Broch

Prawn farming

Spade Cultivation

Stones of
Calanais (Callanish)

Loch
Langavat

Stornoway
Lews Castle

Eye Peninsula
An Rubha)

Point of Stoer

Eddrachillis
Bay

Arkle

Loch
More

Me

Scarp

North Harris
(Ceann a Tuath
Na Hearadh)

Kebock Head

Enard
Bay

Loch
Assynt

Freshwater Lochs

Suilven

Taransay
(Tarasaigh)

Toe
Head

Corran Ra sandbar
Corran Sheileboist

Scalpay
(Eilean Scalpaigh)

Shiant
Islands

Summer
Isles

Ullapool

Little Loch Broor

Sound of Harris

South Harris
(Ceann a Deas
Na Hearadh)

THE MINCH

Pabbay
Berneray
(Eilean Bhearnaraigh)
Boreray

Renish
Point

Lochan
Seatga

Fionn
Loch

Lochan
Fada

North Uist
(Uibhist Atuath)

Loch
Snizort

Basalt columns

Kilt waterfall

Loch
Torridon

Loch a'
Chroisg

Little
Minch

Heiskar
or
nach Islands

Hornish Point

Benbecula
(Beinn Na
Faoghla)

Rona

Gairloch

Rudha
Hallagro

SKYE

Portree

Raasay
Inner
Sound

Sound of Raasay

Loch Maar

Loch
Mullardoch

South Uist
(Uibhist a Deas)

Scalpay

Kyle of
Lochalsh

Eilean Donan Castle

Broadford

Loch
Cluaine

14

Barra

Eriskay

BRIDES

Canna

Soay
Cuill

Sound of Sleat

Loch Hou

A　B　C　D　E　F　G　H　I　J　K　L　M

Lyness　Flotta　St. Margaret's Hope

Pentland Firth　North Walls

SOUTH RONALDSAY

Dunnet Head　Island of Stroma　Brough Ness

Whiten Head　Strathy Point　John o' Groats

Duncansby Head

Thurso　Castle of Mey

Loch Hope　Tongue　Loch Calder　Sinclair's Bay

Loch an Dhèrue　Loch Watten　Noss Head

The Burn of Lyth

Loch Meadie　Loch Naver　Sinclair & Girnigoe Castles

Wick

Loch nan Clàr

Loch Ghòire　Lybster

North

Loch Shin

Sea

Loch Brora　Helmsdale

Lairg　Beatrice Oil Platform

Brora

Loch Fleet　Golspie

Bonar Bridge

Dornoch

Domoch Firth

Tarbat Ness

Tain

Loch Morie

Alness　Invergordon

Loch Glass　Cromarty　*Moray Firth*　Burghead　Lossiemouth

Dingwall　Findochty　Portsoy　Rosehearty

Findhorn　Buckie　Whitehills

Muir of Ord　Fortrose　Nairn　Cullen　Kinnaird Head

Fort George,　Forres　Banff　Macduff　Fraserburgh

Beauly　Moray Firth　A96　Elgin

Inverness　Culloden　Aberchirder　New Pitsligo

Mormond White Horse

Rothes　Keith　Turriff

Lochindorb　Craigellachie　Dufftown

Urquhart Castle　Loch Ness　Wind Farm　Grantown-on-Spey　Aberlour (Charlestown of Aberlour)　Huntly　Ellon

Oldmeldrum　Colliesto

Tap O'Noth

Carrbridge　Rhynie　Mons Graupius Battle Site　Inverurie

Loch Mhòr　Kildrummy Castle　Kintore

Aviemore

15

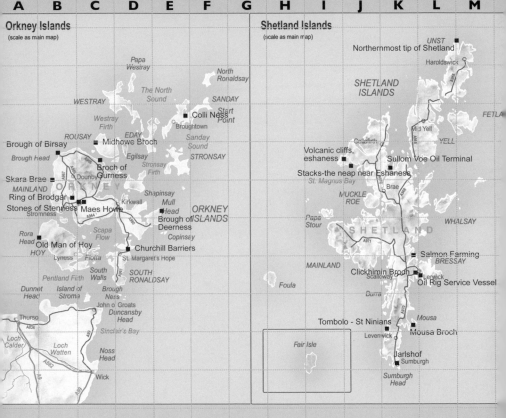

Orkney Islands
(scale as main map)

A B C D E F G

Papa
Westray

The North
Sound

WESTRAY

Westray
Firth

ROUSAY
■ Midhowe Broch

Brough of Birsay ■

Brough Head

Skara Brae ■
Dounby
MAINLAND
Broch of
Gurness

Ring of Brodgar
Stones of Stenness ■ Maes Howe
Stromness
ORKNEY

Kirkwall

Shapinsay

*Mull
Head*

EDAY

Egilsay

*Stronsay
Firth*

*Sanday
Sound*

STRONSAY

North
Ronaldsay

SANDAY

*Start
Point*

■ Colli Ness

Broughtown

ORKNEY
ISLANDS

Brough of
Deerness ■

Copinsay

*Scapa
Flow*

Rora
Head
Old Man of Hoy ■
HOY
Lyness   *Flotta*

■ Churchill Barriers

St. Margaret's Hope

Pentland Firth

*South
Walls*
SOUTH
RONALDSAY

*Dunnet
Head*
*Island of
Stroma*

Brough
Ness
John o Groats
*Duncansby
Head*

■ Thurso

Sinclair's Bay

*Loch
Calder*

*Loch
Watten*

*Noss
Head*

Wick

Shetland Islands
(scale as main map)

H I J K L M

Northernmost tip of Shetland

UNST

Haroldswick ○

*SHETLAND
ISLANDS*

FETLA

Mid Yell

YELL

Collafirth

Volcanic cliffs,
eshaness ■

Sullom Voe Oil Terminal ■

Stacks-the neap near Eshaness ■

St. Magnus Bay

Brae ■

*MUCKLE
ROE*

WHALSAY

*Papa
Stour*

SHETLAND

Foula

MAINLAND

■ Salmon Farming
BRESSAY

Clickhimin Broch ■

Scalloway   *Lerwick*
Oil Rig Service Vessel ■

Durra

Tombolo - St Ninians ■

Levenwick

Mousa

■ Mousa Broch

Jarlshof ■
Sumburgh

*Sumburgh
Head*

Fair Isle

Distances from the north-eastern tip of mainland Scotland:
Kirkwall, Orkney: *37 kilometres (23 statute miles)*
Fair Isle: *130 kilometres (81 statute miles)*
Lerwick, Shetland: *204 kilometres (127 statute miles)*
Northernmost tip of Shetland: *278 kilometres (173 statute miles)*

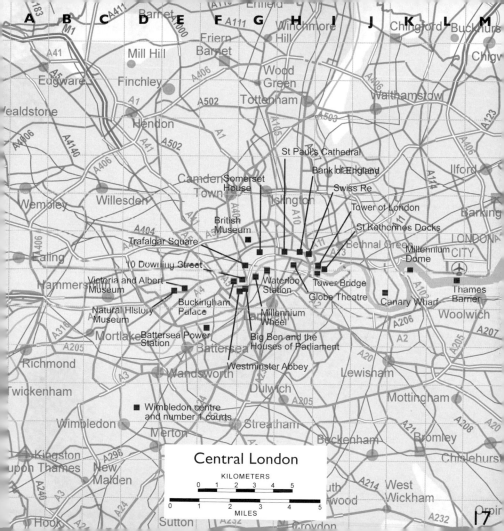

Central London

Central London

A B C D E F G H I J K L M

Edgware
Mill Hill
Finchley
Friern Barnet
Barnet
Enfield
Winchmore Hill
Wood Green
Tottenham
Walthamstow
Chingford
Buckhurst
Chigwell
Wealdstone
Hendon
Camden Town
Islington
Bethnal Green
Ilford
Barking
LONDON CITY
Wembley
Willesden
Ealing
Hammersmith
Mortlake
Richmond
Twickenham
Wimbledon
Kingston upon Thames
New Malden
Hook
Sutton
Merton
Wandsworth
Battersea
Dulwich
Streatham
Beckenham
Croydon
Lewisham
Mottingham
Bromley
Chislehurst
West Wickham
Woolwich

St Paul's Cathedral
Bank of England
Swiss Re
Somerset House
Tower of London
St Katharine's Docks
British Museum
Trafalgar Square
Millennium Dome
10 Downing Street
Victoria and Albert Museum
Tower Bridge
Globe Theatre
Thames Barrier
Canary Wharf
Natural History Museum
Buckingham Palace
Waterloo Station
Battersea Power Station
Millennium Wheel
Big Ben and the Houses of Parliament
Westminster Abbey
Wimbledon centre and number 1 courts

KILOMETERS
0 1 2 3 4 5

MILES
0 1 2 3 4 5

17

List of photographs with page numbers and map references

THE AUTHORS

ELIZABETH LOVING grew up in south London and has worked in publishing for many years. Her interest in landscape history and agriculture led her to study the relationship between people and the places they inhabit. She has recently completed a degree in Environmental Psychology at the University of Surrey, and is currently examining how the quality of the environment affects the happiness and wellbeing of individuals and communities. She lives in the New Forest – an environment ideally suited for anyone with an appreciation of the natural world.

DAVID HALFORD was born in Germany and spent part of his early life in Africa and Asia. The thirty years he spent in the world of academic and general reference publishing, on both the sales and editorial sides, have taken him to many parts of the world, giving him a keen appreciation of different cultures and traditions. Now working as a writer and aviation photo-journalist, he also maintains his long-standing interest in history and archaeology, with a particular interest in the Roman World. He lives in London and the New Forest.

ADRIAN WARREN has been making wildlife and environmental films worldwide for over thirty years, for the BBC, IMAX large format and National Geographic, and as an independent for his own company, Last Refuge Ltd. As a professional pilot, he specialises in aerial photographic work, and has devised a special wing mounted system for film and video cameras. His many awards include a Winston Churchill Fellowship; the Cherry Kearton Medal from the Royal Geographical Society; and film awards include the Genesis Award from the Ark Trust for Conservation; an International Prime Time Emmy; and the Golden Eagle Award from New York.

DAE SASITORN is from Thailand. She came to England to do a postgraduate study in chemistry many years ago, then had a change of heart to follow her love of nature into the natural history film-making world. She manages Last Refuge Ltd, together with its photographic archives and created the company website. In addition to aerial photography, she undertakes scanning, post-production of images and designs these books.

ADRIAN and **DAE** are currently building a comprehensive aerial photographic archive of Britain. They have published several books including **England: An Aerial View** (2004) and **England: The Mini-Book of Aerial Views** (2005), with new titles on Scotland, Wales and London planned for 2009.

LAST REFUGE Ltd was established in 1992 to document and archive the natural world through films, images, and research, and to play an educational role in raising public awareness in conservation. The company started publishing books in 2004, and regularly supplies images and film from its growing archives to other publishers, broadcasters and interested parties worldwide.

Other aerial titles available from Last Refuge

– *England: An Aerial View, ISBN: 0-9544350-2-8, publication date: December 2004*
– *England: The Mini-Book of Aerial Views, ISBN: 0-9544350-5-2, publication date: November 2005*
– *The Living Coast: An Aerial View of Britain's Shoreline, ISBN: 978-0-9558666-0-9, publication date: November 2008*

Also available from Last Refuge

– *Unseen Companions: Big Views of Tiny Creatures, ISBN: 0-9544350-4-4, publication date: May 2007*

All photographs in these books are available as high quality prints from www.lastrefuge.co.uk